We're
with
Nobody

truth truth truth truth truth truth truth truth truth truth truth truth truth truth t
truth truth truth truth truth truth truth truth truth truth truth truth truth truth t
truth truth truth truth truth truth truth truth truth truth truth truth truth truth t
truth truth truth truth truth truth truth truth truth truth truth truth truth truth t
truth truth truth truth truth truth truth truth truth truth truth truth truth truth t
truth truth truth truth truth truth truth truth truth truth truth truth truth truth t
truth truth truth truth truth truth truth truth truth truth truth truth truth truth t
truth truth truth truth truth truth truth truth truth truth truth truth truth truth t
truth truth truth truth truth truth truth truth truth truth truth truth truth truth t
truth truth truth truth truth truth truth truth truth truth truth truth truth truth t
truth truth truth truth truth truth truth truth truth truth truth truth truth truth t
truth truth truth truth truth truth truth truth truth truth truth truth truth truth t
truth truth truth truth truth truth truth truth truth truth truth truth truth truth t
truth truth truth truth truth truth truth truth truth truth truth truth truth truth t
truth truth truth truth truth truth truth truth truth truth truth truth truth truth t
truth truth truth truth truth truth truth truth truth truth truth truth truth truth t
truth truth truth truth truth truth truth truth truth truth truth truth truth truth t
truth truth truth truth truth truth truth truth truth truth truth truth truth truth t
truth truth truth truth truth truth truth truth truth truth truth truth truth truth t
truth truth truth truth truth truth truth truth truth truth truth truth truth truth t
truth truth truth truth truth truth truth truth truth truth truth truth truth truth t
truth truth truth truth truth truth truth truth truth truth truth truth truth truth t
truth truth truth truth truth truth truth truth truth truth truth truth truth truth t
truth truth truth truth truth truth truth truth truth truth truth truth truth truth t
truth truth truth truth truth truth truth truth truth truth truth truth truth truth t
truth truth truth truth truth truth truth truth truth truth truth truth truth truth t
truth truth truth truth truth truth truth truth truth truth truth truth truth truth t
truth truth truth truth truth truth truth truth truth truth truth truth truth truth t
truth truth truth truth truth truth truth truth truth truth truth truth truth truth t
truth truth truth truth truth truth truth truth truth truth truth truth truth truth t
truth truth truth truth truth truth truth truth truth truth truth truth truth truth t
truth truth truth truth truth truth truth truth truth truth truth truth truth truth t
truth truth truth truth truth truth truth truth truth truth truth truth truth truth t
truth truth truth truth truth truth truth truth truth truth truth truth truth truth t
truth truth truth truth truth truth truth truth truth truth truth truth truth truth t
truth truth truth truth truth truth truth truth truth truth truth truth truth truth t
truth truth truth truth truth truth truth truth truth truth truth truth truth truth t
truth truth truth truth truth truth truth truth truth truth truth truth truth truth t
truth truth truth truth truth truth truth truth truth truth truth truth truth truth t
truth truth truth truth truth truth truth truth truth truth truth truth truth truth t
truth truth truth truth truth truth truth truth truth truth truth truth truth truth t

We're with Nobody

Two Insiders Reveal the Dark Side of American Politics

AlanHuffman

MichaelRejebian

WILLIAM MORROW

An Imprint of HarperCollins*Publishers*

HarperCollins books may be purchased for educational, business, or sales promotional use. For information please write: Special Markets Department, HarperCollins Publishers, 10 East 53rd Street, New York, NY 10022.

FIRST EDITION

Designed by Michael Correy

Library of Congress Cataloging-in-Publication Data is available upon request.

ISBN 978-0-06-201577-8 (pbk.)

12 13 14 15 16   OV/RRD   10 9 8 7 6 5 4 3

In our jobs, we're with nobody.
This book is for everybody.

We're
with
Nobody

1

Alan

It's a balmy summer night in the rural countryside near the North Carolina–South Carolina line. This guy Joey, or Jamie—I've forgotten his name—sits in the dark on the deck of his trailer, silhouetted against the flickering light of a TV that's blaring an old episode of *Married with Children* through the open door. I don't know him and he doesn't introduce himself or even get up from his chair when I approach, but I'm sure I'm in the right place because he doesn't seem surprised to see me. He just says, "Hey, how's it going?" like we're old friends. I pull up a plastic lawn chair and get out my notebook. As my eyes adjust, I notice he's got a shotgun cradled across his lap.

Until now we've spoken only by phone and our conversations have been brief and a bit cryptic, but he starts talking a blue streak before I've even pulled my pen from my pocket, and soon I'm blindly scrawling notes and don't have a chance to ask about the gun. Excited as he is, he's speaking so softly that he occasionally gets drowned out by the obnoxious laugh track on TV, like he's afraid of being overheard, though we're alone in the middle of nowhere. I'm tempted to ask him to turn down the volume because it's hard not to listen to Al Bundy's drivel, but I'm hesitant to interrupt.

I watch the red dot of his cigarette arc between the arm of his chair and his lips as he holds forth about a feared local businessman who's running for

Congress. The red dot flares momentarily; he thumps his spent cigarette off the deck, then lights another. In the flick of his Bic I catch a glimpse of his face. He looks weary for his relatively young age. It appears that life has not been easy for him. I notice these things only in passing, because I'm not here to get to know the guy. I'm here to find out about the congressional candidate, and he supposedly has the goods.

My partner, Michael, and I do this for a living. We're opposition political researchers, which means we're hired by campaigns to compile potentially damning profiles of candidates. Our lives during the campaign season are a coast-to-coast series of behind-the-scenes interviews and paper chase sorties—clandestine missions that revolve around facts, truths, lies, surprises and dead ends, all bundled together with strands of strange situations, odd confrontations and the unique social scenery of the American landscape. One day we're in New Orleans, staring cross-eyed at court records in the hazy morning aftermath of a late night on Bourbon Street. The next we're in New York City, resolutely standing on the last nerve of a records clerk who frowns as she looks at the request I've just handed her.

The New York City clerk episode was typical of the way we approach our job and how our work is frequently perceived. In that case, the records clerk asked, "So, who did you say you're with?" knowing full well I hadn't said. For some reason, Michael and I live for these small moments, when someone, knowingly or not, throws the gauntlet down.

"I'm not with anybody," I replied, knowing that if the clerk had blinked, the questioning would end. But we were in New York City, where institutional blinking is rare.

"What do you mean, you're not with anybody?" she persisted.

"Well, technically, I work with him," I said, tilting my head toward Michael, who was leaning against a wall, texting someone and half listening to a conversation he'd heard a hundred times before. He glanced up just long enough to give her a little half-assed smile and a wave that actually looked more like he was dismissing her. She frowned again and turned back to me.

"So why do you want this?" she asked.

I just stared at her. All I was asking for were some straightforward tax documents, public records deposited in her office for anyone—for all—to see.

"I mean, what are you going to do with it?"

"It doesn't really matter, does it?" I said. Because it didn't, and she knew it. This is America. What we were looking for is part of the public record, and why we wanted it was nobody's business but our own.

Though Michael and I are, technically, with someone, in that we provide the information we compile to someone who, in most cases, is associated with the Democratic Party, that's largely immaterial to the completion of our work, and it's irrelevant to anyone else. We're essentially free agents, and how we go about doing our work is up to us. Our personal and professional ideologies are reflected only in who gets our reports. We want our guys to get elected, and achieving that involves more than uncovering damaging information about their opponents; it means doing it to our side, too. It's not only about discovering what's impolitic; it's about finding the truth.

Sometimes we focus on private clients, such as a business, but our forte is researching candidates for elective office, using documented records to flush them out into the open. People call it dirt digging, but the dirt is just one by-product of discovering what makes a candidate tick. The search also requires us to navigate the larger issues of the day—immigration, the death penalty, the outsourcing of collectible Snow Baby factories—at very close range. You think of politics as taking place in the seats of power—county courthouses; city halls; state capitals; Washington, DC—but important scenes also unfold at less obvious locales, such as mobile homes on lonely gravel roads where someone who lives on the fringes deigns to tell what he has seen and heard.

We've been doing this for the better part of two decades now, gathering political intel during a weird, extended road trip that no one else would ever take, through America's main streets and back roads. We're guided, more or less, by the conviction that no one is fit to lead unless proven otherwise. Though negative campaigning is often perceived as a bane of politics, we like to think of ourselves as seekers of the truth. In our view, documenting that truth is more crucial than ever, when today's news is prone to distortion, willful ignorance and lies; when untruths go viral in the blogosphere overnight and even conventional media sources give airtime and print space to erroneous claims and rumors; when the headline on the lead story on Yahoo! News about a descendant's account of a ship officer's experiences reads: TITANIC RELA-TIVE REVEALS "TRUTH" ABOUT SINKING. "Truth" is a word that should never be qualified. It's like pregnancy; it's yes or no. It is possible to inculcate the public with untruths or distortions, but as Senator Daniel Patrick Moynihan reportedly once observed, "Everyone is entitled to his own opinions, but not his own facts."

Considering how blithely the truth is often regarded today, Michael and I sometimes feel like relics of a simpler era, gathering our old-timey facts while everyone else obsesses over imaginary death panels and whether the president is a Muslim—a bit of "news" that Obama, regardless of what you think of him, correctly characterized as part of "a network of misinformation that in a new media era can get churned out there constantly." Our primary aim, aside from earning a living, is to help guide the political debate through the real, documented world, where talking points are derived from actual facts rather than from voices emanating from a planet far, far away. We do listen to those voices now and then—you never know where clues will be found—but our work is utterly dependent on locating the documentation.

Unfortunately, that's not always the thread our own campaigns are looking for. Because we usually profile both our candidates and their opponents, to ensure that our side knows how we could be attacked and what we're up against, we get to see everyone naked, for better or worse. Sometimes our guys look good going in and turn out bad; in one case we found that our young, articulate candidate had numerous arrests in his record, including a DUI and throwing a pipe bomb at a high school homecoming parade float. And sometimes the opponent looks bad going in and turns out good. We don't pull any punches in the assessments we ultimately provide to our campaigns. We present our findings, based on the records, then abdicate control and move on.

The guy with the shotgun falls into the category of a deep background source because he professes only to have leads. He has no documentation to support his allegations, which is fine with me. We mostly work under the radar, for a lot of reasons, not least of which is that the truth can be painfully shy. Leads such as these are sometimes dead ends, but they're just as likely to point us in the right direction, toward the documented truth.

Until now our research of the local candidate, a successful businessman, has been shaping up fairly routinely, but the guy with the gun used to work for him and claims that while on the job he uncovered evidence of an arson fire that garnered the man a hefty insurance settlement. According to this guy, the businessman had paid someone to burn his business for the insurance money. He describes how the business was losing money, then says, "Now, watch this . . ."—a phrase he uses frequently, though after the first false alarm I quit expecting there to be something to actually watch. It's just a conversational tic. He's trying to frame things for me, to keep me focused.

I notice that each time headlights appear on the gravel road that curves past his darkened trailer the guy sits up straight, positions his hands on the gun and watches the car or truck crunch slowly past, then picks up where he left off. Who knows if any of what he's telling me is true, but when he alleges that the candidate's social sphere is riddled with criminals, I take the opportunity to ask about the gun. He answers, almost apologetically, that he's afraid someone might try to kill him for talking to me. OK, I say, go on. I'm thinking that the presence of the gun, the anxious car-monitoring, the chain smoking and the obliviousness to the blaring of *Married with Children* could be signs of psychological disarray, but they could also mean he's on to something. It's a question Michael and I often face: Is the source knowledgeable or, well . . . crazy? The answer usually lies in the documentation, if there is any. We've learned to go with the flow even when the flow gets a little strange, because meaningful things happen out in left field, too. It pays to keep an open mind.

As newspaper reporters back in the eighties and nineties, as opposition researchers and as generally curious people, we've come across our share of misfits over the years: people obsessed with this or that conspiracy theory, or who relate some highly original fantasy that is, essentially, a nimbus of hoarded neurotrash—like the man who kept insisting that Michael come over to his house to see the pony that President Reagan had left in his yard, or the woman who believed the federal government was monitoring her movements by strategically placing a dwarf to spy on her in every restaurant she entered. Who but the federal government could afford the payroll for so many dwarves? Sometimes it's best to follow the lead wherever it takes you, at least until you know whether you're chasing the truth or Reagan's pony.

We operate on two basic premises: Only documented facts truly matter, and everyone knows something we don't know. The guys in the asylum in *One Flew Over the Cuckoo's Nest* may have been clinically insane but they knew what Nurse Ratched was up to, and because no one listened to them her crimes went undetected. Everyone has a piece of the truth, and even if it's lodged alongside imaginary ponies or contradicts a piece that someone else holds, it's possible to approximate the whole, to arrive at verisimilitude, by carefully assembling the disjointed fragments into your own mosaic. If that sounds like an entirely unscientific method for proving facts, it is. But it occasionally does lead to documentation. It's like a trial. One witness says this, one witness says that, and eventually the jury picks and chooses what to believe and makes its proclamation. The verdict is afterward officially accepted as the truth. The defendant ceases to be an accused murderer. He's either acquitted or he is a murderer. It's there in print, in the local newspaper, in the courthouse records. It's documented.

There are exceptions. People get exonerated through DNA. Official records contain errors. Paper trails are intentionally hidden or even obliterated. But documented records are the closest society comes to establishing the truth, and if a source's story isn't true it almost always comes apart once you start asking how to nail the paperwork down. Without documentation, or even evidence of document tampering, our investigations go nowhere. We're oppo guys, not the FBI. As such, we're essentially a hybrid species—part investigator, part critic, part paid informant.

From our perspective, much of what passes for political debate today is arrested at the trailer-porch conversation stage. It's interesting, as far as it takes you. If it takes you only to an Internet echo chamber, it's useless for our purposes. Unfortunately, in today's political environment, the documented facts are often left backstage, where they gather dust; while half-truths and untruths—always enthusiastic, able performers—enjoy the limelight. This is nothing new. As Mark Twain observed long ago, "A lie can travel halfway around the world while the truth is putting on its shoes." But it does seem more pervasive now, when there are more and better delivery mechanisms and people seem less enthralled with honest accountability.

For all these reasons, I give the guy with the gun credit for at least having ideas about where the supposedly incriminating records can be found. He says he's willing to talk about it now because he's disturbed by the prospect of the candidate gaining significant public power. He wants people to know what this guy's really like, even if that means putting himself at risk.

The candidate, who projects the image of a familiar mainstream political persona—a camera-ready, outwardly upright, successful businessman who speaks to the values of the district's conservative voters—is, according to this guy, actually a ruthless and vindictive power monger. He concedes that some of the putative crimes would be impossible to prove, which has the effect of making his allegations more credible to me. Though none of this has come out in the media and no charges have been filed, I take his claims seriously if only because he seems to grasp the importance of proving things. Not everyone does.

"I don't know how I got in the middle of this shit," he says. "Know what I mean?" I nod, but I don't. I have no idea how he got into this shit.

We end up talking late into the night, and the next day I head to the courthouse, to the sheriff's office and to other local records repositories, where I find documents that roughly parallel his narrative. But before I'm able to make any definitive links, the campaign waves me off, which is something that happens more often than you might expect, particularly if they're confident of winning the election. Despite the proliferation of attack ads, many campaigns are uncomfortable directly initiating a scandal even if it seriously damages the opponent. In this case the campaign had trepidations about my talking to the guy with the gun at all, and discouraged me from doing so, but I couldn't resist. They want to know everything they can but are fearful of being linked to trouble if it isn't absolutely necessary. I don't even mention to the campaign that some guy has been following me in a Lincoln Town Car as I make my rounds.

Soon, though, word about my investigation starts to spread and everything gets a little freaky. A supporter gets wind of it and promises a scoop to a local reporter. Someone else leaks an incomplete (and not entirely accurate) version of the story to a competing reporter. No one, as yet, has any documentation, and the story that's leaked contains enough obvious flaws to deter further investigation by the skeptical local media. It turns into a mess, really. Our candidate grows increasingly restive over the idea of being caught probing the dark side, of being identified as the source of the allegations, so he puts an end to this line of questioning. Ultimately, he doesn't need to pursue the allegations. He wins. The public never knows what went on behind the scenes, and I never know whether what the guy with the gun says is true. Michael and I are merely pickers in the field. Everything in our baskets belongs to the campaigns.

It's rare for our research to lead us into such troubling zones, but we tend to relish the sketchiness when it happens—which, I suppose, makes us a bit unnerving to others. We enjoy the process of deciphering documentary patterns and reading about telling episodes, but there's nothing like seeing a drama, or even a dramatic aside, unfold before your own eyes. It brings the story to life.

Opposition research is a crucial underpinning of American politics that tends to be obscure by design. It's no secret that campaigns research their opponents, but few people have a clue as to how it's done or who does it. In fact, it's a multimillion-dollar business that utilizes keen-eyed malcontents—who roam the country with a focused political agenda and an abiding love of aberrant details—alongside consultants, pollsters and other political operatives, to piece together their own and their opposing candidates' profiles. Usually there is at least a feeling that we're all on the same side.

Political research is about searching for evidence of both hypocrisy and nobility on front porches, in smoky conference rooms, and in courthouses, bars, deer camps and roadside cafes. It can be grueling, corrosive, satisfying and entertaining by turns. It comes in cycles, gearing up in spring, usually starting with a phone call. From that point on, all bets are off. Whether or not the pollsters end up using our findings to quiz people who still have landlines, Michael and I are out there, tapping the source, piecing together the odd and meaningful political story of America.

After we've completed our research we submit a report to beleaguered campaign staffers who typically stay on the phone all day, subsisting on coffee and fast food, and who, during the rush of the season, have more interest than time. Campaign people are generally hard to impress, though the fact that a gun appears as a prop in our subsequent report is remarked on, favorably in some quarters, because it indicates that we left no stone unturned.

Once the campaigns digest our reports, we undertake whatever follow-up research they deem necessary. The results, when significant, are then introduced into the fray, forming the basis for poll questions, news conferences, direct mail pieces or TV ads. Whether or not the information gains traction is beyond anyone's control because the electorate—you, your family, your friends and enemies—can be a fickle bunch. There's also the question of the efficacy of the delivery. Either way, we rarely hear what happens after we leave town.

Much of our work is straightforward research, but we do occasionally find ourselves in the middle of an outsized drama that's being staged at a small, out-of-the-way venue, as is the case here, and likewise during a Mississippi race, where we ended up being tailed for a day and a night by three good ol' boys in a rusty pickup truck. The appearance of the good ol' boys—who looked like extras from *Mississippi Burning*—offered a reminder that when you're in the business of looking for trouble, trouble sometimes comes looking for you.

The guys in the pickup made their cameo after we stumbled upon documents that hinted at questionable activities by another opposing candidate, for whom, presumably, they worked. We unearthed the incriminating records at a county courthouse set in the center of a stark, small-town square where most of the employees were clearly on the side of the guy we were going after—a familiar scenario. It's not unusual for us to have obstacles thrown in our path, and we can usually detect a hostile dynamic right away. We saunter up to the counter, ask for the voting history of a local power figure, and, based on the reaction we get, may as well have asked, "How long after a person dies can you successfully harvest their organs, bearing in mind that there's no air-conditioning in the cabin?" Yet for every roomful of uncooperative clerks there's almost always one who takes the opposing view, who has perhaps been on the losing end of the power figure's activities or who, for whatever reason, resents him. We always keep an eye out for this person, just in case.

In the Mississippi race, we sized up the situation immediately. The moment we requested the candidate's property tax payment history, everyone in the office looked up. One of the clerks rose from her desk, grabbed a notepad, glared at us and purposefully exited the building. I watched through the window as she strode to our car and wrote down the tag number. Another clerk, meanwhile, demanded to know, "Who are you with?"

Clerks such as these, under the misguided impression that they work for elected officials rather than the taxpayers, can come up with all sorts of ruses and bureaucratic barriers to fend off public scrutiny. This being a small courthouse where the candidate clearly held sway, his minions were unusually bold. Fortunately, this also meant that the process of hiding potentially incriminating records had been sloppy. The minions had grown complacent. Probing the deed books on our own we found that the candidate had, on more than one occasion, bought land with another man, both of whose names appeared on the original deed of sale. But he had sold the property by himself, so that only his name appeared on the deed transfer. The deed irregularity could have been innocent enough—some kind of verbal agreement, perhaps—but it also could have been a method for transferring money to the candidate without accountability. We made copies of everything under the watchful eyes of the clerks, at least one of which, using history as an indicator, was secretly cheering us on.

Later, as we were driving to the interstate hotel near the Alabama state line where we planned to spend the night, I began receiving strange calls on my cell. At first no one spoke. Then a stranger, without identifying himself, asked where we were and hung up when I refused to say. I still don't know how they got my cell number, but soon after, Michael's then-wife called to say that someone who refused to identify himself had phoned their home to ask where we were staying that night, saying he was working with us, which made her suspicious. We generally work alone, and anyone associated with one of our campaigns invariably knows how to reach us. All of which served to put us on guard. It is moments like these that make us tolerant of a stranger bringing a gun to an interview. Sometimes it's not just paranoia.

I tend to be pretty observant, but I was downright vigilant as we neared our hotel. I took note of the extras from *Mississippi Burning* when I saw them sitting behind us at a traffic light, and observed that they were still behind us when we turned on to the frontage road at the next intersection. As we checked into the Hampton Inn they entered the parking lot and backed their truck into a spot facing the registration desk. I made a point of letting them see me see them as we headed to our rooms, but they didn't seem to care. When we went to dinner they were still out there, in the parking lot, and they followed us to the restaurant. When we emerged from the restaurant, they were parked under a streetlight, staring in our direction, and they proceeded to follow us back to the hotel. It occurred to me that their tailing skills were subpar, unless they'd been told to be obvious about it, in hopes of scaring us off. I also wondered, "All of this over some questionable land sales?" Given their level of commitment, it seemed likely that our suspicions were justified, and that there could be more going on. When some of these guys run for office, it's like they wake up one day and think, "Hey, there's some power over there, waiting to be tapped—my own little honey hole." They don't seem to grasp that public power is subject to public scrutiny—in this country, at least. We want to say, "Hey, look over here. We see you!" The *Mississippi Burning* guys served only to reinforce the feeling that we were on the right track.

The next morning, as we were preparing to depart our hotel, I noticed that the good ol' boys were gone. Rather than feel relieved, I was more wary. I wondered what had become of them. Then I had an idea. It didn't seem beyond the realm of possibility that they could have planted something—a tracking device or, I don't know, a bomb?—under the hood of our car. I know it sounds paranoid, and maybe it was, but one thing we've learned is that there's always someone who wants to blow someone else up, literally or figuratively. Whether they follow through has to do with the person's attractiveness as a target, the availability of a suitable delivery mechanism and proximity.

As Michael was about to start the engine I told him to wait, to pop the hood. Not being a morning person, he gave me a withering look.

"What? So you can look for a bomb?" He started laughing, mocking me. Then he stopped laughing, said, "OK," and popped the hood.

We got out and peered into the engine compartment. I'm not sure what, exactly, an improvised explosive device might look like—maybe some frayed wires running from the starter to a cartoonish six-pack of dynamite? There were lots of hoses and wires. I didn't see anything that looked suspicious. I considered checking the oil, since I was there anyway, but decided against it. Apparently the good ol' boys had only wanted to worry us. I slammed the hood, we got back in the car and drove over to the Denny's for an awful breakfast, where I overheard a kid in the next booth (who was having ice cream for breakfast) ask, "What's 'thankful' mean?"

Searching for car bombs is not a step we normally include in our research itinerary, just as we don't normally encounter people with guns, but the plot frequently turns and the general outline we follow is necessarily fluid. We always start with the same basic plan, but because every place and every race is different, we never know where we might end up. It actually helps that we are, to a certain degree, perennial outsiders, removed enough from local politics to be willing to ask stupid questions, yet familiar enough with the usual kinds of political shenanigans to know what to look for. It's also crucial, obviously, to keep track of the reactions of people around us. In some cases the opponent runs for cover once word gets out that you're triangulating around a potentially damaging revelation. You find a crack in his or her record, a sliver of light escapes and they drop out of the race or their supporters head for the hills. Alternatively, you may get a counteroffensive, which can take the form of threatening phone calls or a news conference attacking our candidate for running a smear campaign.

Unfortunately, the pathology of misdirected ambition isn't limited to political miscreants. We see it to varying degrees, in myriad forms, in many of the candidates we research, including some of our own. It comes with the territory, with the desire to lead, to wield power, to earn the adulation of others. Everyone, it seems, likes good head. The big question is where does that ambition take them? Where they stand on the issues is what matters, but sometimes the best way to determine that is to document their behavior across the line. When our discoveries turn the attention on us, and occasionally summon nervous guys with shotguns or paralegal thugs, it becomes glaringly apparent that what we're doing matters.

In the end, the Mississippi campaign used some of what we found, though the big issue was a detail that at first had seemed innocuous, compared with the suspicious property transactions: the fact that the opponent was operating one of his personal businesses from his official government office. I recognized this during a routine records search.

He ended up losing the race, and afterward vanished from the political scene.

The other candidate, the one who supposedly was involved in the fire, fared somewhat better. Though he lost the congressional election, he found a future in politics on the lower end of the scale. I will never hear what happens to the trailer guy. Like so many people in the realm of politics, he is a bit player. He matters for a moment, then the political process rolls inexorably on, carrying Michael and me toward the next location on our itinerary and whatever revelations it may bring.

2

Michael

She seems at ease, sitting on the top step of a large front porch, her legs crossed and a long, slim cigarette between her fingers. She wears a bit too much makeup, perhaps, but her face is pleasant and gives no reason to believe that the ensuing conversation won't be the same. But then, that's what I always think.

"So, can you tell me a little about your ex-husband?" I ask, standing on the bottom step with a notepad and pen in hand.

She just stares back, a blank expression at first, then a look of thoughtfulness as she searches for the right words. She has a soft voice and a demeanor that leaves me wondering whether she really wants to say anything at all. Then, in a tone that could put a baby to sleep, the words come, and for a moment seem as if they'll never end.

Cocksucker. Cheating son of a bitch. Selfish bastard. Asshole. They are in sentences, of course, but all I hear are the words. I try to display sympathy and concern, but inside I'm smiling because I know, as I always have, that ex-wives, ex-husbands, ex-girlfriends, ex-lovers, ex-anythings make some of the best sources.

Alan and I had received the call a few days earlier. A local politician was making noise about jumping into a congressional race against a longtime incumbent worried about his record and, apparently, about his job. The election was more than a year out and the potential opponent had not yet announced. The task at hand was to try to make sure he never did.

We get these projects every now and again. Just see what's out there, they say, and if there's nothing, so be it. But of all the different types of campaign research we do, for some reason these usually prove the most fruitful: local politicians rattling their chains without having thought through the whole idea—and without understanding that longtime incumbents work hard to remain longtime incumbents.

The initial response from the ex on the front porch is a great start. But I need considerably more detail to go along with her most eloquent string of profanities. If we don't have documentation, we have nothing. I know that her ex-husband likely isn't a true "cocksucker," and if he were, that wouldn't be a crime. Even a congressman busted for soliciting sex in a Minneapolis airport bathroom can walk away with only a disorderly conduct conviction under his belt.

The point is just to keep the conversation flowing, to keep asking questions and always, always show interest in the answers, even if they are of little value. For more than a decade as newspaper reporters, Alan and I asked questions—a seemingly endless string of questions that sometimes led to great stories, but more often than not simply retrieved the information needed to meet a deadline and please an editor. The ability to always be the asker and never the answerer is a powerful thing. To always get and never give may seem selfish to some, but offering information to gain information diminishes its value and weakens the interviewer. Questions are a companion; they are a friend. And the more ways you know how to ask them, the more successful you will be.

Unfortunately, in this case, the front porch interview isn't going very far. It's not because she doesn't want to offer as much as she can; it's because she just doesn't know that much about the man. His business dealings are a mystery to her. His political affairs are an unknown. She knew him as a husband only, and now she despises him.

"So when you say he's a 'cocksucker,' I'm just guessing you're talking about your marriage?"

And then she begins. Yes, she is referring to her marriage. Yes, he was the shittiest, most ill-tempered husband on the face of the earth. Yes, he had put business and politics before her. And yes, he had left her and started seeing another, younger, woman. That little piece of trash, as she refers to her.

It was not a lot of useable information, but enough to keep going. "Can you tell me anything about her? About their relationship?"

They now live together, she tells me. The girlfriend doesn't work, doesn't have children. They travel a lot, go to places he never took her when they were married. She resents him for all of it. Fury tempered by hatred.

"Anything else?"

"Oh yeah," she says, almost as an afterthought, "I think he was arrested for beating her up."

These are the moments when a pause is not only mandatory; it is involuntary. It gives you time to take a deep breath and let the words wrap themselves around you. You betray no excitement, no indication that the statement has any more meaning than any other. Reactions are contagious; they have the potential to frighten and shut down the recipient. So I just stare down at my notepad and jot the words "assault" and "arrested." I scribble a big star to the side.

"So, what was that all about?" I ask in near monotone, still looking down. "Was there anything to that?"

She proceeds to tell me that the couple was going on a vacation when the incident supposedly occurred. She doesn't know where they were going, somewhere out West she thinks, but says he "slapped her around" in an airport en route. I gently probe for additional details, but she doesn't have much else. She must have recognized that the information held some value because she then asks if it is something I think I can use. I tell her it's possible, but that I'm not sure.

But that isn't true. I am sure.

Polling is the lifeblood of any well-funded political campaign. The information Alan and I provide is used to develop the questions that pollsters ask of voters. And one thing polls show is that voters will tolerate and even accept an awful lot of misgivings by politicians. They have tolerated cheating spouses, dalliances with prostitutes, the occasional DUI, college drug use and even cocksucking in the White House. But they will never condone domestic violence. Slapping a woman around is a political killer.

Back at the office, I'm poring over a U.S. map, trying to figure out where the slapdown may have occurred. The red circles in front of me highlight the major airport cities that the couple could have passed through en route to a vacation out West. They are starting points for tracking down the alleged assault. If such an incident did happen, there could be an arrest report or at least an incident report on file at one of those airports.

"You might be better off just taping that to the wall and throwing darts at it," Alan tells me, unnecessarily.

"No, I have a system," I say. But in reality the trail from the ex-wife's front porch is leading nowhere. I am striking out, one airport at a time. With only a couple left to go, I know if they don't pan out, then we have nothing. And we have to have something.

If exes make the best sources, cops are often some of the worst. They, like us, deal in collecting information, not disseminating it. They don't talk much, especially to people they don't know. It's even harder when the conversation is by telephone. And oftentimes, criminal acts aren't made available to the public until they enter the court system. Arrest and incident reports may never see the light of day. But you still have to try.

The call to the next airport security office starts the same way the others have. I tell the officer that I'm trying to track down some information on an assault that supposedly occurred in front of one of their gates. I have the name of the assailant and the victim, and I'm hoping for some assistance.

"What do you want this for?" he asks.

"I'm doing some work for a client who needs to track this information down for a project they're trying to resolve in a hurry," I say. Clear, yet confusing.

"Who's your client?"

"I'm not at liberty to say."

At this point, if the officer asks for additional details about the incident, you're usually golden. This one asks if I have the date of birth of the man I'm inquiring about. Of course I do. I got it from the pissed-off ex-wife. Do I have a date this happened? No, just a period of time during which it supposedly occurred. Do I know what happened? Uh, no, that's what I'm asking you.

He seems somewhat satisfied and asks for my phone number. He's going to do some checking and get back to me. Good, but not guaranteed.

The thing about campaign research is that you never really know what you're going to find until you find it. For me, that's the fun part. It's like playing a slot machine—a past but pleasant money-losing diversion from work that most often left me wondering why I hadn't just saved time by tossing hundred dollar bills out my car window before even getting to the casino. But of course the real thrill didn't come from winning money. It was that split second before the reels aligned to reveal victory or defeat, that moment before my eyes told my brain whether the third symbol was another 7 or just a BAR.

Clients and campaigns, however, don't care about split-second thrills or the moments before. They want the goods, and they want them yesterday. They want them scanned and e-mailed or faxed—preferably the former. So while I wait for my callback from airport security, I'm explaining to a third-party contact—a campaign go-between—what I've found, but what I don't actually have. It's a fun conversation, especially for Alan, who rolls his eyes when he gets to hear the same lines for the umpteenth time.

"Yes, that's what she said happened."

"No, I don't have anything yet to prove it."

"Yes. I'm trying to get it."

"No, if it's not there, we don't have much else."

About this time another call comes through on another line and Alan picks it up. It's the airport guy, so I quickly hang up and prepare for the reels to stop where they may.

People have a tendency to want to join in on the good fortune of others, especially when they believe they are the source of that fortune, however indirect. I suppose it's just human nature. You feel satisfaction, so they feel satisfaction; you can hear it in their voices. The security officer is considerably more animated on the call back and he's excited to share because he's found what I am searching for.

Yes, there is a report of an assault that occurred in one of the terminals—Concourse Bravo, he calls it—between the ex-husband and the girlfriend. It apparently began with an argument that evolved into a shouting match and escalated into the slaparound. There was a busted lip, some blood and a short trip to the carpet for the girlfriend. Although the report doesn't mention how or if the case was resolved, and makes no reference to an actual arrest, it is better than I had hoped.

Alan and I do not relish the pain or misfortune of victims. If you ask us, a man who's responsible for that kind of abuse should get everything that's coming to him and probably more. But it's not for us to decide. Our job is simply to find, document and collect. The judges and juries lie within the voting booths and campaign offices.

Like anyone who enjoys his job, we take pride in our work and feel a certain sense of gratification when the task at hand results in success. So when the now-helpful airport security officer says he will be glad to fax the report to our office, I feel good.

The client or candidate for whom we work generally has the next move. With a report like the one we've just provided, the scenario might go something like this:

A mutual friend of both the incumbent and his potential opponent makes a friendly visit to the potential opponent and explains that a "situation" has arisen that could cause him some embarrassment and bad publicity. The friend offers a few details about the incident and says it would probably be better if he considered backing off his intentions of running against the incumbent. At this point, the potential candidate acts surprised and insists he was not involved in any such incident. He tells the friend that he has every intention of running. His insistence quickly turns to silence when the friend pulls out the incident report and hands it to him.

Within a couple of weeks of passing along the faxed report from airport security, Alan and I get an e-mail telling us that the ex-husband has decided, in so many words, to stay put.

"Did you read this?" I ask Alan, almost in passing.

"Yep. Pretty good," he responds without looking up from his computer. Nothing more is said.

During a campaign season, Alan and I walk through dozens of airport terminals, and every time I pass through Concourse Bravo, I'm reminded of front-porch exes and the things they know.

3

Alan

Two plainclothes cops in an unmarked patrol car roll to a stop in front of the Jersey City train station and motion for us to get in. As I open the back door, Michael whispers something that I don't fully understand, other than the words "make it back." I don't really need to hear the rest because I'm pretty sure I'm thinking the same thing: We're breaking the law just by getting into this car. I hope we make it back uneventfully.

The last time I climbed into the back of a police car, I was in my early twenties. It was during an ice storm, in the middle of the night, and the defroster had gone out on my old Camaro as I drove through a crime-ridden neighborhood in my hometown. Eventually a solid sheet of ice formed on my windshield and I was forced to abandon ship and make my way through the bitterly cold streets of the hood, underdressed and shivering, hoping the criminals were hovering around space heaters inside their lairs. When a police car swooped to a stop beside me, I rushed to open the back door and get in, which seemed to surprise the cops. They turned on the inside light and stared at me.

"It's warm in here!" I said, relieved to be in from the cold. They exchanged a glance. The driver proceeded to report to the dispatcher on his radio, and the other cop told me they'd stopped to pick me up for questioning, because I matched the description of a man who'd just robbed the Green Derby Lounge. They were pretty sure now that it wasn't me, on account of how I was so eager to get in the car. There was a lesson in that, I figured.

I'm not sure what the lesson will be this time around, but I know that unless you're a beat reporter on assignment or a refugee from an ice storm, it's a safe bet that something's wrong any time you find yourself in the backseat of a cop car. If you haven't broken the law, well . . . actually, you probably have broken the law. Cops are supposed to arrest criminals, not squire political operatives around.

The guy who summoned us to Jersey City had said over the phone that someone would meet Michael and me at the PATH station, but I hadn't anticipated this. It's early in the campaign season—March, when we start meeting with the people to whom we propose our oppo projects. There's usually an air of excitement because we're at the front end of a potentially enlightening and important project. Something is almost certainly going to happen, and you have no idea what. The campaigns are nascent. Few of the key positions have been filled.

During the first meeting, which may take place in person or by phone, we listen to someone (typically a recently arrived campaign manager) recite what he knows about the candidate and the opponent, after which we explain what, specifically, we propose looking into, along with our fee. Then we wait for them to decide whether they want to proceed, which can sometimes take months.

We'd expected this meeting to be a familiar brainstorming session, but from the look of things, it's going to go a little differently. We had already noted that there didn't seem to be a campaign manager, and it wasn't clear if there's even a campaign organization. Yet they—whoever they are—were champing at the bit to get started. The guy on the phone had said that they wanted to go after this one elected official, and his reasons for doing so were vague. Now that we're here, I don't really like the idea of being chauffeured by two plainclothes cops to an unknown destination, to meet with someone we don't know and whose agenda is unclear. I'm sure everything will turn out fine, but I can't help feeling a little uncomfortable.

On some level, Michael and I are always kind of waiting for something to go wrong. There's serious stuff beneath the surface of politics, and some of these people, they're not only irascible, they're dangerous. Added to that, our nerves are already on edge after being subjected to three aborted plane landings at the Newark airport in a terrific thunderstorm the night before. Michael says he's feeling a bit dehydrated—a condition he falls prey to more than most—and now we both feel the strange sensation that we've entered a deleted scene from *On the Waterfront* and we aren't sure how it's going to play out.

"Thanks for the lift," I say, far too cheerily for Michael's taste, judging from the look on his face as we pull away from the curb. "You guys doing OK today?"

The guy riding shotgun mumbles yeah. The driver just glances back at me in the rearview mirror. There are no formal introductions.

We drive silently through dilapidated blocks of closed Jersey City businesses, many of which are marked by rusty signs and tagged with gang graffiti, illustrating the final gasps of what appears to be a long socioeconomic lament. Sprigs of economic life appear here and there, but for the most part it's a wasteland, replete with beggars representing all the nations of the Earth. It's new to us, and interesting in a depressing way, so we peer out the windows and take in the scenery.

The silence seems to be to everyone's liking, particularly Michael's, who is annoyed by what he describes as my penchant for trying to engage everyone we meet. These guys don't really need to know why we're here and likely wouldn't care if they did, and it doesn't seem prudent to ask why or how two cops came to be chauffeuring us around. I'd actually like to know, but everyone seems to agree that the less said the better. It's one of those moments where you realize the oppo could easily be turned on you. I imagine a judge or a reporter asking, "Did you not think there was anything unusual about using a police cruiser for your personal taxicab? Did you consider the illegality of this arrangement you'd entered into?"

"You need anything before we get there?" one of the cops asks.

After ten minutes of driving in silence, during which I'd tried to memorize the turns we were making as we passed through the run-down city, the question catches me off guard. I point to Michael in the rearview mirror and say, "Yeah, actually, my friend could probably use a bottle of water. He's been a little dehydrated since the plane trip yesterday." Michael responds to this thoughtful request by shooting me one of his "what the hell?" looks. Though he knows it's true, I might as well have said, "My little buddy here is thirsty."

The driver whips in front of a bodega, double parks, his partner darts inside and then returns with the precious liquid. He won't take Michael's money. We pull away, round a corner and come to a stop at our final destination, a row of warehouses on the waterfront.

At the tinted glass door that leads inside we're met by a guy dressed in an actual pinstripe suit. With bushy eyebrows and a prominent mole on his cheek, he looks like he's come straight from wardrobe. He introduces himself and ushers us down a long hallway and into an actual smoke-filled room where several other men sit around a small confer-ence table. To my relief, they do not look particularly menacing. On the contrary, they look like they've all just been rejected at a casting call for *The Sopranos* and aren't at all happy about it. The fellow who brought us in, whom Michael and I later secretly nickname Mo on account of the mole, tells them we're the guys who are going to find out what they want to know. They appear unimpressed.

The scene in the meeting room is stereotypical of how many people envision the backrooms of politics, but it's actually a departure, even for us. Our work is routinely strange, and takes us places we'd otherwise never go. Whether it's in a smoke-filled room on the Jersey waterfront or someone's cozy den in rural Kansas, we approach each situation the same way: We listen to what the campaign people have to say, and we look for signs of trouble. Still, we like to start with a genial parlay, something that apparently is going to be denied us in this case. It feels like we're being hired to take someone out, literally, and the bosses have no interest in knowing any more than they have to about us.

In a sense we *are* being hired to take someone out, which is some-thing we'd be cool with, oppo-wise, were it not for the suspicious and slightly condescending attitudes of whoever these people are. There still have been no introductions, and certainly no informative backchat about their individual roles, which is usually one of the first pieces of information we get. There's also the nagging feeling that this group may be amenable to breaking the law. They have agreed to our fee, though, so our only concern is that we not break any laws ourselves or benefit from their being broken by others.

Opposition research can be expensive—tens of thousands for a congressional campaign or hundreds of thousands of dollars for a presidential campaign—which is why it's most often used in big-ticket races. But if the money is there, oppo may be done for statewide and even smaller races. Well-funded organizations, including some in New Jersey, have been known to spend whatever it takes to prevent any opponent from taking office, down to the local school board level. The fee may be paid by a national party, an individual campaign, a third-party group, a party caucus or, as is the case in Jersey City, a private donor. Non-campaign sources are sometimes used to avoid public revelation of the expenditure by the campaign itself, because there are still people out there who are shocked to hear that a candidate hired "an investigator," as they put it, to "smear" their opponent. So much for our belief in political transparency.

The problem in Jersey City is that they—whoever "they" are—are secretly going up against a powerhouse who, once he finds out, will not respond with a petulant news conference about their disgusting, un-American smear campaign. He'll turn loose the hounds.

As they sit impassively around the table, I explain that the core of our work involves examining the candidate's documentary record: newsclips, lawsuits, criminal record, his education, personal affairs, finances. "That, and anything else you might think it prudent for us to look into," I add. Their response is to stare at me blankly, as if to say, "Are you done talking?" This is something of a relief; who knows what else these guys might think it prudent for us to look into?

Before they can add anything, I start to elaborate on our usual MO. Some things I expect will be of little interest to these guys, but they matter just the same, such as votes cast by incumbent lawmakers and whether they, themselves, take the time and interest to vote in public elections. We also look at campaign contributions and at government contracts that may have been awarded as a result (I expect this to pique their interest, but their expressions don't change). We review what's been reported in the media about them, and at what they say as opposed to what they do. In short, we take every piece of documentation of a candidate's adult life, tie the most politically significant parts together and put it all into context for the campaign to use to sway a voter.

Even as I explain this to the guys, I'm imagining that the process of piecing the guy's record together will result in some awkward encounters; for that matter, just getting to this point required us to pass through several disquieting portals, beginning at the Newark airport. As passengers screamed and we were thrown against our seat backs again and again, I managed to retreat to a sort of Zen state, which Michael very much resented because he was about to explode.

As I talk, I glance over at Michael, who's clutching his bottle of water like a talisman and staring at Mo. He's only too happy to let me do the talking. Throughout the rest of our trip, he will find it difficult to fully recover from the aeronautic and meteorological shock to his system delivered on the way to the Newark airport. As he will remember it, New Jersey was an affront before we even touched the ground, which—we being contrarians at heart—will be useful, in its way.

I can already envision how this will go. Each morning at breakfast Michael will catalog the difficulties we face and reiterate his abiding desire for a smooth, uneventful flight home. The die has been cast. This is good, I tell myself. An anxious, dissatisfied Michael is a dogged oppo-researching Michael. Being in a foul humor for four days will spur him on.

After I turn the floor over to Mo and his cohorts, and they tell us about the candidate they want researched, I see the look on Michael's face and realize we're both thinking the same thing, again: The trouble here may actually be right in this room. It seems a fight has erupted over who holds the absolute power in their little political fiefdom and these guys have decided that they do, despite the fact that as far as we know they don't even have a candidate. They've just got a political vendetta. To make matters worse, it soon becomes apparent, based on what they tell us, that the target of their anger could squash them like the skittering cockroach that Mo suddenly and vengefully flattens with a loud smack of his shoe on the conference room floor, causing everyone to jump.

As they finish telling us about everyone the big guy has corrupted and/or destroyed during his political career, Michael and I realize the cards are stacking up against them.

"Are you sure you want to do this?" I feel obliged to ask.

From the response I get, it's obvious that circumspection is not a strong suit with these guys. They stare at me, not even bothering to ask what I mean. I begin to explain my concerns, but one of them quickly cuts me off. They are well aware of what's at stake. End of discussion.

They then lay out a fairly half-baked strategy, telling us to pay particular attention to the officeholder's voting record, which actually comes as something of a surprise because it sounds legit. I'd have been less surprised if they'd said they wanted us to stake out his car-crushing business down by the river. They don't really know what they're looking for, or even how they intend to use it. They just know they want to know what there is to know. Mo tells us they need a quick turnaround (none of our clients ever wants a leisurely turnaround) and, without further ado—no one even rises from his chair, much less offers to shake our hands—sends us on our way, back outside to our waiting police car.

The cops are leaning against the back fender, smoking cigarettes. As I open the door to get in, I glance over my shoulder and see the Statue of Liberty in the distance—her back, appropriately enough—which is something I hadn't noticed coming in. I see Michael looking at it as well, and I know we're thinking the same thing: This is America. As weird as politics may be, as cutthroat as it can become, as entangled and seemingly nonsensical as it sometimes is, there's no place where it works better.

Driving back to the PATH station I tell myself it doesn't matter whether we like these guys. We deal in actualities. The guy we're researching is not an enemy. We don't even know him. Our job is simply to discover and evaluate the facts. Whether there's a silver bullet that's going to put him in his political grave is beyond our control; we can only make our best effort. It makes no difference how much a campaign or a guy with a mole wants us to find something if there's nothing useful to find. But when you go after a guy with the clout that this New Jersey officeholder carries, you better be prepared to go all the way, because the consequences of timidity or incomplete action can be devastating.

As we undertake our research over the next week, we find that the guy has a decades-long voting record, a lengthy list of campaign contributors and a host of personal financial records to plow through. We eventually tie him to legislative efforts that may have exploited the atmosphere of crisis in the post–9/11 world, which would require a lot of spin to get traction. He also has a questionable record on immigration as it relates to homeland security, for what that's worth. Like many politicians, he has accepted large campaign contributions from industries he's helped through support for various pieces of legislation, and has taken big chunks of money from developers whom he's assisted with government subsidies. But this is New Jersey, for God's sake. Rather than feel relief when Mo suggested we look at his voting record, we should have recognized the reality of the situation—that when guys like Mo and his cohorts plan to hang their hat on something as mainstream as a voting record, there probably isn't going to be much there.

Two weeks after our waterfront meeting, we wrap up our final report. There's some good stuff there, but honestly, not enough to make a serious dent in the candidate's political future—not in a place like Jersey City. The big ones may fall harder, but slinging a rock heavy enough to bring them down takes a lot of muscle. Our guys, we soon find out, don't have it. I'm finishing up the report and Michael's been on the phone with them for only a few minutes when he hangs up and says simply, "Forget about this. We're done."

"Cold feet?" I ask.

He shakes his head. "They said it didn't matter anymore, but yeah, they got scared."

"Did you tell them we'd already finished the report?"

"They didn't care," he says. "And one more thing: They're not going to pay us."

"Oh, they'll pay," I say. "We'll see to that." Our business mantra is: We always get paid. Who wants to make enemies of the oppo guys? We've got all the inside information.

A few weeks later, after we've gotten a lawyer friend to send Mo a very carefully worded demand letter, Michael makes a follow-up call. It's very brief, and at one point he appears to be cut off in midsentence. Then he slams the phone down.

"What'd they say?" I ask.

"Well, they basically told me if we wanted the money we could come back up there and try to get it," he says. "I'm thinking we probably won't do that."

As it turns out, the Jersey boys had neither the balls nor the wherewithal to bring the big guy down, and as far as they're concerned, we're lacking in the same departments when it comes to going after them. It's true; we relish neither the thought of getting further entangled with the Jersey City political machine, nor going to court, and thereby publicizing the fact that we went after a big-name politico. We'd probably lose anyway.

In fact, Jersey City remains the only instance, to date, that we've been stiffed on a major job. We later read that one of the guys in the smoke-filled room had been charged with taking bribes. At least he got paid.

4

Michael

Our friends don't generally understand what we do. Saying "political research" doesn't adequately explain how Alan ends up being placed under guard in a municipal office, or how I spend a late night in a basement watching a candidate's ballroom dancing skills. Neither of us is known for being particularly enthralled with politics in our normal lives; like many Americans we glean our political news from *The Daily Show*. We don't watch C-SPAN. From our perspective, most of what passes for political discourse in the country today is dry, didactic, self-important, shrill or sensational, tinged with a new type of radicalism that often makes little sense. Even worse, much of it isn't based on facts, or even on what Stephen Colbert calls "truthiness."

We're not in the political debate business, though we often find ourselves being dragged into debates when someone discovers that our jobs have something to do with politics.

"So what do you think about the new Supreme Court nominee?" someone will ask me at some party.

"Never easy to choose one," I say.

"Don't you know it'll be bad for abortion opponents?"

"I haven't really thought about it," I answer. "But the Saints seem to be doing great this year. Do you think they'll get to the Super Bowl?"

Alan can be even more off-putting. I've watched him being asked a political question, think for a moment as if on the cusp of an answer, and call me over, saying, "Have you met my business partner, Michael?" Then he promptly walks away, leaving the cycle to begin again.

Politics for us is confrontational only during our on-duty hours when the responsibilities of the job often demand it, such as with the New York clerk. And though we do house opinions on many issues, we don't generally share those with others. To do that introduces a dynamic in which no one ever wins. When we're working, we rarely feel any ill will toward the parties involved. Neutrality is key to objectivity regardless of party affiliation. Like Michael Corleone told his brother in *The Godfather* right before he shot two people dead, "It's not personal, Sonny. It's strictly business."

Have Alan and I ever had some in-depth conversation with one another about our political philosophies? Not that I recall. That doesn't mean we think or even live the same way. Alan resides in the country in an 1830s plantation house; I live in a downtown high-rise. He has a keen eye for the repetition of history as it relates to government and politics. It may look like something new, he'll say, but beneath the surface it's simply a reconstituted version of the same old picture show. Between the two of us, he is probably the more liberal, which likely stems from the fact that I was raised in a staunchly conservative Republican family in a Republican city in a Republican state. To this day, my family will tell you that they still don't know what happened to me. Yet, some of that upbringing has stayed with me, providing a useful balance to an occupation that could lend itself to one-sided values.

Alan and I tend to see things a little differently from most people, in part because we just see things differently and in part because of the nature of what we do. For us, oppo is about human nature as much as politics. It's mostly an excuse to scrutinize ambitious people, to fully reveal their stories down to the most awkward details, all while getting to know America, and the unique and sometimes strange people who inhabit it, one pointed question at a time. We like rolling into towns unannounced to ask those pointed questions, from Miami to Seattle and points in-between, and we like occasionally going off track, such as when we got lost in a creepy neighborhood outside Cincinnati where the streets are lined with small, doll-like houses that from all appearances are inhabited exclusively by aging, shirtless fat men who sit on tiny porches and stare at nothing.

Being opposition researchers has freed us to research a range of characters—in some ways, even more so than in our previous lives as daily newspaper reporters. We've become immersed in a side of politics that tends to remain hidden from public view: the process by which candidates are systematically dissected, evaluated and prepared for potential public attack. There are fundamental differences between what we do and investigative reporting, of course. We don't need a firm lead to justify undertaking our investigations, and we do not publish the results of our work. Though we have a clear agenda, in that we're beholden to our campaigns, we're free agents when it comes to uncovering the truth. We're deeply vexed by what Colbert calls the "fact-free zone" and are, of necessity, relentlessly objective, because there's no need for sycophants in the realm of opposition research.

Everything we cite in our reports must be thorough, honest, accurate and, as we can't stress enough, documented. Whether our candidates know it or not, the last thing they want is for us to bowdlerize their record, or to have the opposing campaign reveal a weakness that we have not discovered first and forewarned him or her about. Despite the obvious differences, and the fact that we contribute to the campaign's portrayal of their opponent's record, our essential objectivity positions us closer to investigative reporters than to spin doctors.

We stick to the facts even when we're tempted to opine, which is difficult when the person we're researching is really out there. It's hard to hold our tongues when a candidate, for example, says of abortion that liberals would take our children and "flush them down the toilet." Or says his opponent doesn't want our children to know about George Washington, Thomas Jefferson and John Adams. Or supports a school abstinence curriculum that advises students to wash their genitals in

Lysol to help prevent sexually transmitted diseases. Those kinds of comments sting us.

Our strenuous reviews of everything from township council minutes to congressional hearings can be as boring as a C-SPAN marathon. Yet there is always the promise of meaningful discovery and of interesting characters—the borderline psychotic clerks, the borderline psychotic candidates, the gossipy waitresses, the hired thugs, the elderly men operating out of a historic jail in Liberty, Missouri, who were clearly intent on controlling our minds. In short, there is always America.

We start each day, as most people do, on the Internet, which is a great source of ideas and leads. Unfortunately, it's also wildly unreliable. You can, after all, edit Wikipedia yourself. We use the Internet as a roadmap and, when possible, a source of documentation, but ultimately, all our information must originate from someplace real—someplace you could actually go if you had the time, inclination and perhaps a rented Hyundai.

Naturally, some of what we gather in the field is later wrapped in colorful cellophane and packed in confetti to make it look tastier than it is. Some of it is rotten by the time it gets to you, and if you're smart you'll immediately throw it out. There are a lot of opportunities for things to go wrong. Do not blame us for any of that. Our hope is that by illuminating the process of opposition research you will be better positioned to cull the good from the bad. Politicians and their minions have been prone to lying since the first ambitious Cro-Magnon jockeyed for control of a mastodon hunt, yet never before has there been a system for broadcasting untruth as sweeping and effective as the combination of television, talk radio and the Internet. It's important to listen closely, and skeptically.

As opposition researchers Alan and I are, admittedly, attracted to lies; we savor revealing them for what they are. But it's distressing to see how political lies have adapted to public scrutiny, much the way shape-shifting infections in industrial hog farms respond to tanker truckloads of antibiotics being dumped into the coursing veins of millions of host swine. The purveyors have become increasingly effective despite increasing access to the facts, in part because of the successful use of dazzle camouflage—whereby complicated imagery is superimposed on the truth to fool the eye.

A fairly recent example of this phenomenon is the candidate in New York who was called to task for sending out mass e-mails containing racist depictions of the president as well as a video of a woman having sex with a horse. You can Google it if you really need to know his name, which, again, is not the sort of information Alan and I typically retain for long. More important than his name is how his campaign responded to the controversy over his e-mail. They characterized the revelation as part of an attack campaign by his opponents, who were clearly more concerned with bestiality than with the real issues of the day, such as the economy. The idea was to associate the problem with the opponent, to cast the messenger in doubt, despite the obvious. In his case, it didn't really work, but it sometimes does.

Arguably, the entire effort to invade Iraq in 2003 was based on dazzle camouflage. Only when the camouflage was stripped away— too late—was the truth revealed, and by then the effort had succeeded, at least in its original intent. And President Bill Clinton undertook numerous high-profile military campaigns (in Iraq, Sudan and Afghanistan) while Congress was debating his impeachment over the Monica Lewinsky affair, and another (in Serbia) after he was acquitted, which some critics said closely paralleled the movie *Wag the Dog*, in which a fictional president uses a fake war to distract the electorate from a sex scandal. (Of course, that movie was reputedly based on President George. H. W. Bush's launching of the Persian Gulf War to deflect criticism of his administration in preparation for a reelection bid.)

Dazzle camouflage is most effective when its practitioners are skilled, when the outrage factor of their infractions is low, or when the voters simply hate their opponent more. In such cases, the candidate can be dressed up as pretty much anything, and no one seems to care. "Dazzle camouflage" isn't something we made up, by the way. The Allied Navy developed it during World War I, when the advent of airplanes and submarines reduced the ability to hide battleships using conventional camouflage. The goal was to trick the enemy's visual range finders through the use of confusing geometric designs that made it hard to estimate the ship's size, speed or direction.

Politically, the goal is to render the enemy—in this case, you, the undecided voter—unsure about what you're seeing, and by extension, about what really matters. Our job is the opposite of this. Our job is to clarify the ship's size, speed and direction; to illustrate, through incontrovertible facts, that this or that candidate has or does not have what it takes to lead you, for very specific, verifiable reasons. This occasionally does require special glasses, but that doesn't mean you can't try it at home.

We view our research through the prism of our background in journalism, because that's how we were trained, but it's up to the campaign whether to make use of that. Either way, our backgrounds influence how we gather information and organize our findings. Most of the time our work is comparatively solitary, punctuated by the odd interview with the candidate, the campaign manager and perhaps an approved source or two. The work itself comes through word of mouth, and it's safe to say that there are only a handful of people who operate the way we do, though there are big names within both parties who sometimes help orchestrate opposition campaigns. It's hard to accurately quantify how often such research succeeds in killing a candidate's bid for office, or, conversely, electing a candidate, because so many factors come into play, but there are a few obvious examples, such as the downfall of presidential hopeful John Kerry as a result of the much-maligned, yet effective, swift boat campaign, and of fellow presidential hopeful Michael Dukakis as a result of the Willie Horton affair. What you may not know is that it has also been used to derail the political aspirations of a guy running for the school board in South Jersey. Oppo is done, literally, all over the map, and in every stratum of politics—if the desire and the money are there.

Opposition researchers have a penchant for discovering weakness, but we also keep our eyes peeled for the rare example of strength, even honor and valor, that emerges from the ruins. Somewhere between roaming the waterfront of Jersey City in the backseat of an unmarked police car, and discovering a guy in the Midwest making loans to his own campaign while simultaneously reducing child support payments to his daughter, we find a different America—an America where anything can happen politically, where a criminal can be reelected mayor of DC and where a caring and dedicated nurse with no political experience can kick ass at the polls. Meanwhile, the rest of the world watches anxiously as the United States veers crazily from one election to the next.

5

Alan

Michael and I happened on the *Palais de Pal* on a warm winter day in 1988, at the dock of a lake that until recently had been a cow pasture in Fulton, Mississippi. Fulton is the seat of Itawamba County, whose claim to fame is that it's the birthplace of Tammy Wynette, though for us it's more memorable as the temporary mooring of the *Palais* and as the location of the Sands Motel, where an impressive stand of old-growth mildew inspired Michael to wear his socks in the shower.

Itawamba County made the national news in 2010 after the school board canceled the high school prom because two female students announced their intention to attend as same-sex dates. After the ACLU filed suit, the school board scheduled what was later characterized as a diversionary prom for seven students, including the lesbians and two students with learning disabilities, while the other kids danced and snapped cell phone pics at a secret location. Good times! So you can imagine that if twenty-two years earlier you had been a disoriented, slightly judgmental and, it must be said, flamboyant houseboat traveler from Chicago, you could have picked a far better place to become stranded.

When we first spotted him, Richard Kinst, owner of the ninety-one-foot *Palais*, was standing forlornly on the deck with his dog, Sheba, a German shepherd mix with her tail curled between her legs. Michael and I were reporters on assignment for the Jackson newspaper the *Clarion-Ledger*, investigating the economic impact of the Tennessee-Tombigbee Waterway, a series of man-made canals and impounded lakes that passed through Fulton on the way from the Tennessee River to the Gulf of Mexico. As we were interviewing one of the farmers who'd built the cow-pasture marina, he noticed us staring over his shoulder at the odd tableau of Kinst and his boat. The farmer rolled his eyes and informed us that the *Palais* had been at the marina for two years, since soon after the waterway opened. We sensed interesting trouble. After dutifully taking down the farmer's statistics regarding the number of boats he'd accommodated in his erstwhile pasture, and wrapping up our interview, we strolled over to talk with Kinst, who turned out to be erudite, witty and starved for conversation.

As he led us on a tour of the *Palais*, Kinst maintained that he'd been in Fulton for one year, not two, the chronological discrepancy perhaps stemming from the farmer's weariness or from Kinst's secret satisfaction with his own misfortune. He rued the day, he said, when he and his captain had selected the two-hundred-mile Tenn-Tom as a more user-friendly route to the Gulf than the notoriously treacherous Mississippi River. Their plan had been to moor the *Palais* in New Orleans and hire it out for "intimate excursions," but things had gone awry in Fulton, the result of an undisclosed dispute. The captain had subsequently abandoned him. Kinst, who seemed to have styled his diction and hand gestures after Gloria Swanson in *Sunset Boulevard*, knew nothing about piloting his boat and was not inclined to learn. He was very noticeably going nowhere fast.

In the farmer's defense, the *Palais de Pal* was kind of creepy. The interior decor leaned toward the macabre, with heavy burgundy velvet drapes, stained-glass windows, gold-plated candelabra, a fake fireplace and a grand piano. It was very dark. Kinst, despite his protests, clearly reveled in the sublime adversity of being marooned aboard his floating palace, and appeared to be further energized when he noticed us taking notes. The truth was finally going to be told. His story was about to be documented. Possibly, even, his captain would read about it in the newspaper. Paraphrasing a line from the musical *A Chorus Line*, he loudly proclaimed, with outstretched arms, as if to embrace the whole sorry state of affairs, "Suicide in Fulton would be redundant!" In the minidrama of his life, everyone in Fulton would, at that moment, stop what they were doing and bend their ears to hear the echo of his lament.

The story of Richard Kinst and the *Palais de Pal* provided us with a perfect opportunity to showcase what the multibillion-dollar Tenn-Tom project really was: a series of flooded farm fields where the most dramatic developments involved costly, quirky asides. At that time, all news accounts about the waterway had been accompanied by standard-issue photos of huge tows of barges. Distributed by the Tenn-Tom promotional board, these photos had actually been taken on the more commercially viable Mississippi River—one of the first examples of dazzle camouflage that Michael and I had come upon. What the promotional board had sought to do, essentially, was make a series of flooded cow pastures look like they were supporting a gargantuan tow of barges headed to an international port. The truth was plainly evident to us during a weeklong boat ride along the length of the route, when we passed only one tow. As an economic development project, it was a $2 billion federal failure. Had you relied on the news releases being disseminated by the promotional board and local congressional offices, you'd never have known. But you would have learned this telltale truth: Six of the multimillion-dollar locks-and-dams were named for U.S. congressmen.

We later heard that Kinst had found a new captain and made his way south to Mobile. After that he disappeared from our screen. I recently Googled "Palais de Pal" and found a boat by that name moored in Green Bay, Wisconsin, but I can't say for sure if it's the same vessel—and don't even get me started on Green Bay.

The point is that we might never have known what a colossal lie the Tenn-Tom represented, nor would we have likely become opposition researchers, had we not taken that investigative boat ride in 1988.

Newspaper reporters are notoriously self-centered and rarely work well together, but the Tenn-Tom proved a notable exception for us. We'd devised the trip with photographer Scott Boyd as a kind of field junket, during which we would travel the route, through numerous locks and dams, in Scott's bass boat, drinking beer and investigating what we suspected from the outset was an economic and environmental boondoggle. Over the course of our journey Michael and I found that entertaining ourselves while working made us more productive and opened us to interesting stories that we'd have missed had we not strayed from the program. It also made the tedium of comparing cost-to-benefit ratios infinitely more palatable, and when it came time to actually write the stories, the division of labor between us developed naturally.

The resulting series encompassed feature stories about characters such as Kinst as well as a charming elderly man who'd been evicted from his ancestral home for a park that was never built, and hard-hitting investigative pieces about the political chicanery that enabled the bogus development project to be built. The Tenn-Tom represented a watershed for us, and not because we ended up winning a hokey in-house award from Gannett, the monolithic corporation that owned the newspaper, but because it showed us how well we worked together— better, in some ways, than either of us worked alone. It also illustrated the utility of peering beneath the public relations veil, and of doing the legwork to bring the story home.

Afterward, Michael and I returned to our respective beats. We remained friends, though a couple of years later I left the newspaper to take a job as an environmental researcher for the state attorney general, and a year after that went to work for the governor as his environmental aide. Michael ended up taking a job as communications director for the mayor of Jackson. After the governor lost his reelection bid and I found myself out of a job, I cobbled together enough freelance writing work to stay afloat. I was chastened by the efficiency of negative politics and had learned a few things about it, and Michael, for his part, was tired of being a political spokesman. So it was that our circuitous career paths led us to go into business together in 1993, to do, among other things, opposition research—essentially, to devote ourselves to delving into otherwise hidden stories against the backdrop of America's massive political machine. A political operative we knew asked if we'd be interested in doing research for a campaign in Chicago, and we jumped at the chance. I don't recall how we decided who would go, but it ended up being me.

In early December of 1993, when the Christmas lights were strung across Michigan Avenue and rosy-faced children hurried down snowy sidewalks with mothers bearing colorfully wrapped gifts, I set off in search of political trouble, my first steps into a darker, overlapping universe. Michael's maiden voyage came soon after and took him to Maryland, where he worked for three weeks on a statewide campaign while making his temporary home in a cinderblock motel.

I no longer remember who the opponent was in the Chicago race, though I breathed, ate and slept with the candidate's history for two weeks. I could perhaps find the name if I had to, such as if I were subpoenaed to testify, but that's not what's relevant here. These politicians come and they go. Michael and I have come to accept the fact that while we fully immerse ourselves in our subject candidates' lives for a time, we tend to forget their names soon after. After eighteen years, we even get confused about where some stories unfolded, and with so many campaigns under way during a typical season, we even occasionally forget where our plane is headed. Fortunately, the documentation we compile serves as an external hard drive. What's important here is that during a routine review of newsclips and courthouse records, I passed through the menacing portal of Chicago politics—a system that vies with New Jersey's and Louisiana's for sheer institutional corruption. I was surprised by how much dirt there was, and not far beneath the surface, either.

Also surprising, to a new opposition researcher, was how people reacted to what I was doing. I remember that the Lebanese cabdriver who drove me in from the airport, who'd fled Beirut during the war, was very much intrigued when he asked why I was in town and I told him I was investigating a politician. He was amazed that it was possible to openly do such a thing. He loved that about America he said. So did I. On the opposite end of the spectrum, I met an attorney in the gym of the apartment building where I was staying who was all chatty until we had a similar conversation. I was concerned that he might know someone involved in the race, so I said I was doing research, the subject of which was confidential, which put him on the defensive. He made some excuse and hurried off. He was the first of now countless people who have seemed threatened by my reticence to talk about my work.

The true revelation regarding the Chicago race came after I returned to the office. I'd come across what appeared to be a connection between the opponent and several people rumored to be involved with organized crime, which, not surprisingly, was extremely difficult to prove. It was only after Michael and I began receiving phone messages from a Chicago number warning us to back off that it became clear we were on to something, which was both exhilarating and unnerving. In the end, the very act of digging sent ripples through the campaign, as word got around that we were researching the opponent's possible mob involvement. Though it's hard to say whether that significantly influenced the election, the opponent lost. I don't remember what Michael found in Maryland, though he still complains about the cinderblock motel and the one small window in his room that looked out on a dumpster.

Soon after that we found ourselves being paid to roam the country, scrutinizing all kinds of politicians. It was like researching and writing an extended series of investigative and human-interest pieces, without the bylines. We were generally aware of the stereotype of opposition researchers—smarmy guys who plumb the depths of society for damaging tidbits about politicians that are then used to sully the political process. To some extent, this is true. But not all of us are smarmy and our work is not necessarily subversive.

We started our business, Huffman & Rejebian, in a tiny office in an art deco high-rise in downtown Jackson that by the time we moved in had become "affordable." We shared a single laptop and took turns sitting behind a desk bought from a used office furniture store—an old metal husk from the forties, scarred and dinged, for which we purchased used aluminum office chairs to tastefully match the period. When we finally got a second computer, we set up our office like a miniature newsroom, facing each other yet shielded by our monitors so we didn't have to stare directly at each other all day. The shielding worked so well that in a subsequent office a friend came in toward the end of the day and remarked to Michael, "Wow, nice shiner!" at which point I realized that I, a professional investigator, had failed to notice that the person sitting across from me for the last six hours sported a black eye. It was like a marriage, in its way; unavoidable familiarity at times made us oblivious of each other.

The rest of our floor was vacant and the hall lights were always off, seeming to emphasize that we were outside the mainstream, which we liked. When we occasionally had visitors we'd hear the echo of their footfalls in the dark, empty hallway before their silhouettes appeared at the frosted glass window of our door, which gave our office a decidedly *noir* atmosphere. It was clear that we inhabited a fringe realm. Similarly, our being located in Mississippi seemed to confer a mysterious, offbeat air on us in the minds of campaign workers in places such as New York and California. We were, in a sense, inscrutable, yet with a reputation for delivering. We had no website, no promotional materials, no cold-call list. Clients came to us through word of mouth only.

There weren't many people doing what we did, and there still aren't, for many reasons, including the corrosive effects of looking for the bad side of everyone and the volatility of the people you encounter, who range from noble public servants to destructive parasites. There is also the seasonal nature of the income. But the main reason is that most people are not that good at getting to the bottom of things. Few people have clear ideas about the origins of . . . well, much of anything. FedEx delivers a fruit basket during the holidays; a link is forwarded by a Facebook friend; someone on TV hurls a rotten tomato or a pipe bomb from an angry crowd. Where, really, do these things come from? Most people don't have a clue. Who has time to try to get to the bottom of things, what with

Sandra Bullock's husband having an extramarital affair? The answer is: We do. We care very much about the origins of the information that fuels negative politics. Once you start gathering that kind of information it's hard to stop, with the result that entire towns occasionally fall under our critical eye, and now and then we turn our wrath on each other.

Starting out eighteen years ago, we worked in total secrecy. Any investigation requires discretion, after all. But the volatility of today's political and media environment has lifted some of the traditional taboos about our line of work. A candidate who can't afford his own researcher may hold a news conference to decry his opponent's having hired a "private detective" to discredit him, but this is a quaint throwback. Most people are now aware that political research is routinely done, and social networking sites have blurred the lines between what's public and private, anyway. On one hand, it can be distressing when someone forwards you an inflammatory, baseless e-mail, but it's also liberating for us as researchers in that people are becoming less easily shocked by our digging.

During a recent research project in Georgia, as I was requesting copies of property tax records for a candidate who'd been late paying numerous times, the clerk came upon one request and said, "This isn't the candidate. You must have written the number down wrong." She knew the candidate, knew what I was doing and was not at all put off or surprised. This is most decidedly not always the case, but the fact that it happened at all represents a minor sea change. In the past, few clerks complied with our requests unquestioningly unless they loathed the candidate we were researching.

When we are confronted by obstructionist clerks and others who attempt to throw obstacles in our path, we gird ourselves with the knowledge that in this, the golden age of lies, we are on the side of truth. If you have nothing to hide, you have nothing to fear from opposition research. Finding out what's going on is about far more than sitting down to Google someone (which, unfortunately, is how many campaigns are coming to view opposition research), or citing an undocumented claim in someone's blog. In the end, the cold, hard, documented facts are our best hope of knowing what's really going on, and the best way to find them is as close to the source as possible. That's something that's understood even in the underworld of recalcitrant clerks. The process of discovering salient facts is crucial to the world's greatest evolving democracy and, at times, is also extremely entertaining—as we learned long ago, while hoisting beers in a bass boat on the Tenn-Tom.

6
Michael

During one of the climactic scenes in 1939's *Mr. Smith Goes to Washington*, Jimmy Stewart's affable character, the newly elected U.S. senator Jefferson Smith, rails at his fellow Senate members that "a certain man in my state, a Mr. James Taylor, wanted to put through this dam for his own profit. A man who controls a political machine! And controls everything else worth controlling in my state. Yes, and a man even powerful enough to control congressmen—and I saw three of them in his room the day I went up to see him!" The voters, Smith insists, have a right to know when politics gets corrupted, and it's his responsibility to tell them.

The idea that negative politics is a recent phenomenon, that once upon a time elections were decided by polite, informed debate, is complete fantasy. Attacking political opponents has been used effectively for centuries. In some cases it's been done honorably; in other cases it's gotten people killed.

Among the earliest evidence of oppo, one of the most dramatic episodes dates to the first century B.C., a tumultuous period during which Julius Caesar was assassinated, a slave named Spartacus led a cinematic uprising against the Roman Empire ("They trained him to kill for their pleasure . . . but they trained him a little too well!" gushed Universal Pictures), and the navy of Mark Antony and Elizabeth Taylor went down in defeat in the Battle of Actium. With so much material to work with, it's not surprising that the debut of opposition research was among the era's milestones.

Of course, it wasn't called oppo at the time, but in the first century B.C., Marcus Tullius Cicero, then the Roman consul, famously documented a plot by one Lucius Sergius Catilina (commonly referred to as Catiline) to murder several senators and overthrow the government. In what would have been the executive summary of his research report Cicero proclaimed, "How long, O Catiline, will you abuse our patience? . . . You do nothing, you plan nothing, you think of nothing which I not only do not hear, but which I do not see and know every particular of." In other words, "Catiline is a scoundrel! It's been documented!"

Cicero charged that Catiline had established an armed rebel camp, that during a secret meeting he and his cohorts had formalized their plot, that two Roman knights had been employed to slay Cicero in his sleep and—to ensure that the story ran above the fold—that Catiline had murdered his wife to make room for another woman while engaging in an act so despicable that Cicero refused to even speak of it. Upon announcing the last detail, Cicero no doubt paused—meaningfully. Everyone was dying to know! Cicero may have been referring to allegations that Catiline had had sex with a vestal virgin, who was said to be the half sister of Cicero's wife, and may have married his own daughter.

Most of what Cicero revealed appears to have been factual, with the possible exception of his claim that Catiline sought to "destroy the whole world with fire and slaughter," which would be pretty tough to document.

Public disclosure of the damning details had the desired effect. When Catiline took his seat in the senate, other senators got up and moved, leaving him a solitary figure on his bench. Emboldened, Cicero called for his execution. In what was essentially history's first documented attack ad, which ran live, Cicero asked, "For what is there, O Catiline, that you can still expect, if night is not able to veil your nefarious meetings in the darkness, and if private houses cannot conceal the voice of your conspiracy within their walls—if everything is seen and displayed?" Perhaps it wasn't catchy, but people caught his drift. Today, "O Catiline" would be the opposition's mantra.

Catiline attempted to respond, but his fellow senators shouted him down, labeling him a traitor. He scurried from the chamber, throwing out verbal threats, as often happens when there's no meaningful rebuttal. In the end he fled north, where he was killed by Roman troops. As a result of Cicero's later attacks, Mark Antony had his hands chopped off and displayed them in a smartly designed exhibit in the forum.

Although it would be centuries before it really hit its mainstream stride, oppo was here to stay. When scandal-mongering pamphlet wars between England's Whig and Tory parties broke out in the eighteenth century, freelance writers such as Daniel Defoe and Jonathan Swift, whose only alternative was to wait tables, were only too happy to stoke the public's political bloodlust with the necessary diatribes (under assumed names). Soon Thomas Paine and Benjamin Franklin got similar gigs in the increasingly raucous political environment of the American colonies.

In the 1800 presidential race of the fledgling United States, incumbent John Adams found out just how vicious oppo could be when his opponent, Thomas Jefferson, accused him of having a "hideous hermaphroditical character, which has neither the force and firmness of man, nor the gentleness and sensibility of a woman." It didn't exactly get people talking about the substantive issues, and the claim itself was apparently undocumented, judging from a web search of "John Adams" + "nude hermaphrodite," which produces a few hits that, while terrifying, fail to support Jefferson's accusation. Adams didn't take kindly to the introduction of his sex organs into the presidential debate, and saw no need to present proof of his countercharge that Jefferson was "the son of a half-breed Indian squaw, sired by a Virginia mulatto father." The name-calling continued: fool, hypocrite, criminal, weakling, atheist, and so on.

To make sure voters weren't confused about who was which, Jefferson secretly hired a cunning, sleazy Scotsman named James Callender, who had earlier exposed a sexual liaison between Alexander Hamilton and a married woman. Jefferson liked what he'd seen of Callender's work, and on his behalf Callender convinced voters that among other things Adams had an overwhelming desire to go to war with France. Prior to Callender's efforts, the electorate had shown limited interest in the subject of attacking France, but afterward became rabid about it. So it goes with sensational, unfounded attacks.

Somewhere along the way the Adams administration imprisoned Callender for sedition, and on his release he approached Jefferson about a job but was rebuffed. In response, he publicly disclosed their clandestine relationship, adding that, oh, by the way, the president had fathered children with one of his slaves. Two lessons can be drawn from this: Friends turned enemies can serve as excellent sources, and it's never a good idea to alienate the oppo guy.

Considering the lengths to which Adams and Jefferson went to portray each other in a bad light, it's curious that Abraham Lincoln got off as easy as he did during his own presidential bid. Obviously, the mores of the time influence whether potentially damaging information about a political opponent is useful in a campaign, but it seems odd that something that has preoccupied Lincoln biographers in recent years—questions about his sexual orientation—caused so little public debate during his political career. Perhaps it's because men commonly slept in the same bed back then, or because people of the era were loathe to openly discuss homosexuality.

According to some historians, Lincoln slept with at least eleven boys and men during his youth and adulthood. Lincoln never denied the practice, and even raised the subject on occasion, but you can bet we'd hear a great deal of conjecture and supposed "facts" if such a detail came to light during a political race today.

Reporter: Mr. Lincoln, I understand you enjoy sleeping in the same bed with other men—a *lot*. Don't you think it's natural that the voters would wonder about your relationships with these men and . . . occasionally, boys?

Lincoln: I slept with them. That is all. With the men it was mostly a matter of convenience, nothing more. Perhaps we discussed politics before drifting off to sleep, or in the early morning hours. I don't recall much of what we discussed in bed when I was a boy. Perhaps Indians.

Reporter: Can you tell me about this Joshua Speed fellow? You two lived together over in Springfield for four years and slept in the same large double bed, according to people we've talked with.

Lincoln: According to which people you've talked with?

Reporter: I can't say.

Lincoln: Was it that Mrs. Pritchard? The landlady with the hairy ears?

Reporter: Let's stick to Mr. Speed. Is he a Republican, too?

Lincoln: He wasn't then. But he is now.

Though Lincoln was never publicly challenged about his bedfellows during his political career, there were whispers about his relationship with a Captain David Derickson, his bodyguard and companion for eight months during the Civil War. The two reportedly shared a bed during Mary Todd Lincoln's absences, until Derickson was promoted in 1863. The relationship was the subject of gossip. Elizabeth Woodbury Fox, the wife of Lincoln's naval aide, wrote in her diary, "Tish says, 'Oh, there is a Bucktail soldier here devoted to the president, drives with him, and when Mrs. L is not home, sleeps with him. What stuff!'"

Such musings were typically limited to private conversations and diaries, but other topics, particularly a man's political dealings, were fair game for the public discourse, and Lincoln did not shy away from doing his own oppo on that. Prior to the Lincoln-Douglas debates, William Herndon, his law partner, reportedly did some dirt digging in the Illinois State Library to collect "all the ammunition Mr. Lincoln saw fit to gather" for his run against Stephen A. Douglas in the 1860 race.

In response, as still happens today, Douglas decried the use of investigators to vilify him, charging that some of his former political allies had secretly conspired to sabotage him and that one group had published a document "in which they arraigned me as having been guilty of a criminal betrayal of my trust." While other senators were attending church, Douglas asserted, they had "assembled in a secret conclave," devoting the sabbath to their own conspiratorial and deceitful deeds. Considering his constituency, it was good stuff, but it didn't help Douglas in the end.

Opposition research crops up in almost every presidential election thereafter, though the actual phrase did not appear until Edmund Muskie's 1971 presidential bid, when newspapers reported that a female Republican volunteer had infiltrated his campaign organization. Soon after, during the Nixon administration, the practice became systemized: The Republican Party began keeping up-to-date files on potential opponents rather than waiting on the campaigns to dig up dirt on them. Nixon, of course, resigned over an episode in which his lackeys broke into the Democratic Party offices in the Watergate building to steal potentially revealing files. Say what you will about Nixon—he was a tyrant and arguably a criminal—but he recognized the importance of facts. In an era when people create them out of whole cloth, and are rarely called to task for it, the idea of breaking into a building to steal documentation seems almost quaint.

Oddly, considering that political research is more pervasive today, and is done on a far grander scale, there appears to be less accountability than in the past, which is one reason Alan and I have become disenchanted with the meanness of the political posturing that grips the nation. Too much is based on undocumented claims and base contempt. We recognize that we're part of a dubious tradition, but as long as the information can be proved true, it clearly serves a purpose. The problem we have with the political fact-free zone—aside from the effectiveness of certain of its purveyors—is that it's counterproductive. It results in an electorate that is, by turns, sanguine and jaded, and it inevitably pushes the debate further from the truth.

Karl Rove, who for us symbolizes the enemy (and not merely because of our ideological differences), is a particularly venal denizen of the fact-free zone. From his days as a college student, when he stole campaign letterhead from a Democratic candidate and printed and distributed fake campaign fliers touting free beer, food and girls; to the "black love child" whisper campaign about John McCain during the 2000 presidential race, Rove has stunk up more voting booths than anyone else in recent American political history. He may liken himself to a protégé of the late Republican strategist Lee Atwater, but even Atwater conceded toward the end of his life that he regretted many of his less scrupulous methods. Atwater had his hand in the now-infamous Willie Horton ad that torpedoed the political career of Michael Dukakis by highlighting how, as governor of Massachusetts, Dukakis had granted Horton weekend passes from prison. At least that effort was based on fact. Horton was indeed a convicted murderer who raped a woman while on a weekend furlough during Dukakis's tenure as governor. Rove, who masterminded the Valerie Plame fiasco and sought to purge U.S. attorneys who didn't meet his loyalty standards, cares only whether a story will further his agenda. He gives opposition research a bad name, which, considering some of the transgressions committed in its service in the past, is saying something.

The irony is that widespread disregard for documenting the truth has come about at a time when access to public records is vastly improved. Every state now has an open records law, which means that if you don't fall for the bluff of the obstinate courthouse clerk you can get your hands on at least a facsimile of the truth, and much of it is easily accessible online. Between access and technology, nothing in politics stays hidden for long anymore. What's strange to us is that as the public has grown more and more jaded by the process, they're still as seduced by it as the Romans were centuries ago. Sometimes the attacks are legitimate and sometimes they're invented, but the stories, true or not, get a life of their own and become a part of history.

7

Alan

I am sitting in the municipal office of a New Jersey township so small and insignificant that it doesn't warrant a single exit off the nearby freeway. I can hear the cars and trucks, a distant murmur of life passing by, as I sit across the table from a bored policeman in the nondescript anteroom of the township office. It's early summer, when our campaign season really cranks up, and Michael and I have hit the road for an extended period of time, going our separate ways for now as we undertake several research projects simultaneously. I'm focused on a diminutive race, an example of how some political organizations strive to ensure that even third-tier opponents stay where they are.

The cop is reading a hunting magazine as I pore through a tall stack of bound township council minutes, the contents of which are both mindnumbing and, for some reason, jealously guarded by the local powers that be. It isn't as if much happens in the council meetings, but all sorts of bureaucratic alarms went off when I asked to review the minutes, which is why the cop is there, reading about recreational deer urine.

Assigning a cop to guard me in the Jersey township was a bit of institutional indulgence owing, perhaps, to the fact that the focus of my work is a minor township mystery. The implication is that I might try to steal the treasured minutes, for some unknown reason, or that my interest poses some other threat for the mayor, which it actually does, though it's not a threat an armed guard could prevent. All they've done, really, is make it slightly safer for others to speed through town on a summer day.

I was doing my best to take a genial approach to the whole situation because the clerk had at least been nice about assigning me a guard. Small public offices don't generally get a lot of strangers who arrive with what appears to be a very specific yet unrevealed interest. When they do, the staff can choose between being accommodating or officious in their efforts to find out what they're looking for and why, and, if necessary, to simply gum up the works. Michael and I can likewise choose between being polite and unforthcoming or impervious and unforthcoming. We typically take our cues from them.

Michael was once similarly placed under guard during a review of education records in Ohio. He reacted by indignantly asking the clerk, "What do you think I'm going to do, stuff them down my pants?"

One wonders, "Who steals education board minutes, anyway?" The implication was that anyone who wanted to review the actions of public officials was somehow a threat. It was about fear of the unknown. For all the administration knew, Michael might have been a schoolteacher, but because they didn't know, they responded with hostility. By contrast, a records clerk he encountered during another race erroneously had the impression that he was some kind of federal agent working on behalf of an ongoing investigation, and cheerfully gave him everything he asked for, saying, "Oh, yes, sir, we can give you that immediately." The clerk also provided him with a personal workspace and did not charge him for what turned out to be a voluminous number of copies.

"When things are going that well, why say anything to the contrary?" Michael told me later.

Because the arrival of an inquisitive, evasive stranger with a Southern accent may represent the most provocative episode of a small township's official day, I give my current clerk credit for at least being sociable, though I'm aware that sociability often masks a hidden agenda.

"You sound like you're a long way from home!" she'd said, brightly, when I arrived at her window with my records request. After a meaningful pause, during which I failed to offer a response, other than to nod and smile, she'd asked, "So what brings you here?"

My answer—"research"—failed to satisfy. So she'd added, as if on cue, "And who are you with?"

I glanced behind me at the empty office, as if checking to see if I was with anyone, and concluded, "Nobody!" Then I smiled and extended my arms in mock surrender. A tiny furrow formed in her brow. I later overheard her telling someone in the back that perhaps I was a journalist who was comparing the institutional procedures of various town councils around the country, which led me to wonder where such a review might find publication. The supposition that I might be someone who studied small-town council minutes for a living had the effect of making my task seem even duller than it already was.

Opposition research can be exciting when you're on to something, but much of the work is like studying for a minor exam. A big part of it involves evaluating voluminous records of meetings by government agencies and ad hoc tree-pruning committees. That said, there's nothing like being bored to lower the threshold for what you find interesting. You may initially resist talking to the computer programmer in the seat beside you as your plane waits in line on the tarmac, but as the wait lengthens to hours, with no sign that you're ever going to take off, it is possible, out of synaptic desperation, to find yourself developing a low-grade interest in the computer programmer's life, including his recent foray into a master gardening class, held in a temporary building at a school currently undergoing sensitive renovation in a suburb of Milwaukee. When was the school built? What style is the architecture? The thumbnail sketch of his life may be a tour de force of forgettable scenes, but each painstaking detail instills in you a growing determination to find something, anything, to chew on.

Michael and I are similarly inspired to take note of documented details we might otherwise have overlooked. A subtle shift in the tenor of the township council discussion about sidewalk repairs or a bored cop reading about deer becomes a source of minor fascination. It doesn't have to be directly related to the task at hand, though that helps. The point is to keep the synapses firing. We search for anything or anyone of note, such as the escapee from *The Twilight Zone* whom Michael and I stumbled upon in an otherwise abandoned office building in Jersey City, where municipal public records were archived. He sat smoking, alone, at his desk, and insisted he knew nothing whatsoever about where the records we were searching for were located, nor about the boxes of moldering documents stacked in the darkened hallways, nor about the whereabouts of anyone who did know or when they might return. Because Michael and I are not easily deterred, even by someone who comes across more as an apparition than a living, breathing government employee, we pressed him for answers. Eventually he exhaled a puff of smoke, waved a hand toward the hallway beyond the door and said, "Help yourself."

I looked at Michael, who had a quizzical expression. We proceeded to poke through the cardboard boxes stacked shoulder-high in the halls, but there was no order to anything. It was a futile endeavor. The archives of this particular government agency were like the memories of an elderly, demented brain. You could root around in there for as long as you wanted, but the odds were against your finding anything useful. Once we decided to give up, we returned to the office, but the employee/apparition had disappeared. I half expected the formerly busy streets to be eerily devoid of human life when we stepped back outside.

In the real world, where there is relative order to the archiving of records (even if they're under lock and key) the challenge is most often to avoid getting lost in a documentary trance after reviewing hundreds of pages of tedious recountings while in solitary confinement. The most important details are sometimes found on antiquated, wheezing microfilm, in boring tax records, or hidden in the coded language of obscure memos. You have to really, really care what people are saying, and Michael and I do. Even so, we still find ourselves wondering, "Is anything happening here?" If the council members do something meaningful, will I even recognize it through the fog of bureaucratic language? It's like being a reporter on the police beat, sleeping with a police scanner on your night stand; after a while, the chatter lulls you to sleep, and you wonder if you'll even notice if something important goes down. But you always do. There's a sudden shift in tone—in the syntax and cadence of the voices—that tells you something consequential is happening, even though the words may be generic and the tone deceptively flat. So it is with the subtly suggestive minutes.

Michael once researched a candidate whose seemingly minor legislative actions had had profound effects on his community. While serving on the city council, the candidate had voted against renewing a permit for a center that provided exercise classes for stroke victims, saying it was detrimental to the neighborhood in which it was located, despite being warned that denying the permit would violate the rights of the disabled. This, again, surfaced in the otherwise mundane minutes of the council meetings. The elected official's response? "It looks like we're playing favorites for some people." Ignoring the needs of stroke victims may not seem like a significant transgression, unless you or one of your loved ones happens to be such a victim. Just because something seems uninteresting at first glance doesn't mean it's unimportant. Sensational stories dominate the headlines, but history also unfolds on page 3B.

The New Jersey township and its mayor are uniformly bland, which puts me in good stead when it comes to forced fascination with the cop and the minute books, as well as with anyone else who might chance to walk through the door. The minutes are basically one long small-font testimonial to governmental minutiae that in all likelihood no other human being has ever read all the way through, and I alternate my bleary-eyed review with random surveys of my surroundings, which steadfastly refuse to produce anything of interest. I search, at regular intervals, for something remotely inviting to the eye, my gaze repeatedly landing on the same overwatered philodendron in the corner, its leaves wilted and edged with brown; the now-familiar plate glass windows, through which a Chevy Citation with mismatched hubcaps is partially visible; and the notices of garage sales and informational meetings about hazardous waste disposal posted by the clerk's window. It's like being stuck in study hall with a math textbook as a kid, staring out the window at the passing clouds with a level of interest that grows in inverse proportion to the slowly suffocating tedium of the numbers. Meteorology—now *that's* interesting! Except that there are no clouds visible through the window. It's just me, the cop, the minutes and the senseless despair of a neglected plant. There are also, I note, spiderwebs in one corner, where the walls meet the water-stained acoustic tiles of the ceiling, and at one point I realize that the Citation has inexplicably disappeared! How could I have missed its departure?

Before long, I'm spending most of my extracurricular time discreetly studying the cop, a stocky, youngish guy loaded down with crime-fighting appurtenances—a flashlight, a pistol, a radio, handcuffs and other curious, jangly things that on the occasion of our initial introduction I had been unable to adequately catalog without seeming suspiciously overinterested. I don't know what it is about cops that makes me not want to seem suspicious when I'm doing nothing wrong. Why couldn't I comfortably look over all the stuff hanging from his belt before we took our seats and the accoutrement disappeared beneath the table? Now I'm left only with occasional, furtive glances at his strangely placid face as he reads, at the radio mic pinned to his collar, at his name tag and his magazine, on the cover of which is a photo of a deer hunter encumbered with the gadgetry necessary for stalking and killing large herbivores.

Unlike the clerk, the policeman doesn't seem to care what I'm up to as we while away the hours in the foyer of the township office, a place you'd not likely visit unless you had a problem with a water main or a marriage license, or were, like me, secretly researching the mayor. Owing to the circumstances, I feel obliged to limit my occasional dialogue with him to small talk, mostly about deer hunting, which isn't easy when you have never actually hunted a deer. I strive to keep my deer anecdotes geographically nonspecific, aside from referencing the deer I'd recently encountered while jogging in a wooded preserve alongside a highway interchange. It helps that the cop seems content to keep our official hookup anonymous, too. The conversational conclusion we will reach, over the course of the day, is that there are too many deer, everywhere.

Midway through my review, after I've made no obvious moves to abscond with the minute books, the cop has become deeply engrossed in his latest hunting magazine and no longer looks up each time I tear tiny shreds of Post-it notes to mark pages in the record books for copying. Of particular interest to me are the notations recounting mayoral cameo appearances in the council minutes. Though the summaries are pretty general, and utterly devoid of conversational nuance, after the second reference I sense a pushiness on the mayor's part as he urged the council to approve a contract for some infrastructure improvement. I can almost feel the electricity in the room as a certain council member, no doubt a perennial troublemaker who grows his own tomatoes, and talks about it, questioned whether the mayor's recommended contractor was the best one for the job. I imagine the councilman raising one eyebrow as he spoke, eliciting an icy stare from the mayor, and I make a note to check the mayor's campaign contributors to see if the contractor is listed among them.

It's at this point, pretty late in the day, that the stasis is broken by the arrival of an interracial couple, walking hand in hand, who have come to the township office hoping to resolve a problem involving a marriage license. Finally, the township office seems poised to come to life. I listen with growing interest as they explain to the clerk the trouble they're having in getting a marriage license, which, I should point out, does not appear to have anything to do with the fact that they are of different races. In fact, I mention their races only because by this point anything even minutely out of the ordinary is, quite simply, extraordinary. The cop, who is likewise bored, absently licking his thumb as he turns a page, also glances up at them. It becomes evident that the couple knows nothing about the process of getting married and that the license problem is bigger than the clerk is prepared to handle, so she summons the mayor, inadvertently providing me with an opportunity to observe my subject in action, unscripted and unaware.

I've been in the area for three days already and so far haven't found much that's of use for the campaign or even for my own entertainment. The former is obviously my priority, but to come up empty on both counts is hugely disappointing. There are some interesting vistas in this part of the New Jersey–Pennsylvania border country, and some cool bridges across the Delaware, and beyond the more densely populated areas the people are agreeable in an unpretentious, blue-collar way, with an obvious appreciation for bad local pizza joints where everyone knows their name. But it's mostly miles and miles of houses clad in vinyl siding, toll roads and, in the comparatively fortunate areas that have access to on- and off-ramps, a predictable succession of chain hotels, Burger Kings and shopping malls. To give you an idea of how the locals do not spend their time, when I stopped at my hotel's front desk one morning, dressed in my jogging togs, and asked the receptionist if she could recommend a running route, she looked at me blankly and said, "I'm sorry. I'm not sure what you mean."

All that's left, after a long day of doing research in such a place, is either to retire to your hotel room or drive across the eight-lane highway to the Chili's bar to watch whatever game is on TV. I do not really follow sports, though I'm easily mesmerized by movement on the screen, and in such situations I must concentrate on keeping up with the score and the names of the teams in case someone saunters up to the bar and asks a challenging question such as, "Who's winning?" It's embarrassing to appear to be watching a game on TV and not even know who's playing. Likewise, it's humiliating to spend three days doing intensive research in a small town and come up with nothing of value or interest. You know there has to be something there. There's almost always something there.

So when the mayor emerges from his office I'm all eyes and ears. I listen, with growing disappointment, as he responds to the couple's interrogatories and entreaties with seeming empathy. He's actually quite solicitous, and seems to share in the prospective groom's bewilderment over the fact that the marriage license fee is greater than the cost of filing for divorce, which strikes the prospective groom (and me) as unreasonable and illogical. The mayor offers no explanation for the difference in fees but advises the couple to speak with the judge about the procedures for getting a license. He then gives them the judge's name and even looks up the phone number, which seems to satisfy them. After the groom-to-be makes a few rambling closing remarks, the couple exits through the cracked plate glass door. The cop and I exchange a glance, which basically says, "I saw that, and I guess you saw that," and return to our respective reading materials. The mayor looks at me as he leaves the room, though he doesn't seem particularly interested. In the bound volume that lies accusingly before me, the township council adjourns for the day.

Back at my hotel room that night, I go through copies of the mayor's campaign finance reports and find that the contractor he had pushed the council to use is there, as are numerous other contractors for whom he oversaw the awarding of comparatively lucrative contracts, which could indicate a conflict of interest. It might not have been that bad if the contractors had adequately done their jobs, but that wasn't the case, as was evident in the notations in the minutes regarding recurring infrastructure problems that kept popping up long after the contractors had supposedly finished.

As the abuse of political power goes, what happened in the tiny township was a small thing. A few contractors contributed to the mayor's campaign, got some work out of it and ended up doing a crappy job. But it represented a failure of government that manifested itself in the failure of concrete sidewalks. Should an old lady carrying her groceries home from the store have the misfortune to trip on a buckled sidewalk and break her collarbone, it would be possible to trace the nexus of the episode to the minute books.

The same was true of the midwestern councilman's vote against permitting a center designed to aid stroke victims. The vote was buried in the minutiae of the minutes, and at first glance might have seemed innocuous, sandwiched between votes on unimaginably boring inside-government activities, and shrouded in sleep-inducing language about property values and the like. But if you look closely, you don't have to be a stroke victim to recognize that the guy has his own agenda, and that, in this case, it doesn't dovetail with the greater public good. Likewise, the congressman who worked for a business that made millions by relying on Chinese labor, rather than the employment force in his home state: Who, precisely, would such a representative represent?

Because all politics is local, the abuse of the system in the tiny Jersey township illustrates a problem we see across the nation, a problem that is cumulative in scope. The same type of systemic abuse that results in poorly built sidewalks in an out-of-the-way township resulted in the failed federal response to Hurricane Katrina. Small opportunities lead to larger opportunities; small abuses tend to escalate. It's all just a matter of scale.

8

Michael

Standing about five foot five, she's a manly woman, troll-like in many ways. And though she might very well reside under a bridge, she works in a local government office in Missouri. From the expression on her face, we can tell this is going to be unpleasant—a trip to the dentist and a prostate exam wrapped into one.

"And what am I going to do for you today?" she asks in a voice that is irritating, frightening and tiring all at the same time.

It's only Tuesday and it's already been a long week of research. All I can manage is to look at the floor and whisper to Alan, "You do this, please. I just can't." The reason I can't is because I know that the request we're preparing to make is going to unleash an unpleasantness so great in scope as to leave only two options: run away or get beaten to death in front of a legion of bureaucrats who might very well join in the bloodletting.

In another situation, it could have been Alan asking me to handle the troll. But I know he's irritated already at having earlier had lunch at a chain restaurant. Alan hates chain restaurants and has been known to drive all the way to another city to avoid them. Don't ask me why that is, but I suspect when he leaves this Earth, his obituary will read: "In lieu of flowers, donations may be made to any restaurant that has no more than one location." One formulated burger and he's ready to rumble.

"Yes ma'am," Alan says slowly. "We're going to need to look at all the campaign finance reports for these individuals." He slides her a piece of paper with the names we're looking for as I stand to the side, nervously sipping a bottle of water. She stares at it for a moment and then asks how many years' worth of reports we want.

"All of them," Alan says, standing firm in preparation for the aftershock.

Of all the documents we examine during the course of a campaign, finance reports—the listings of the individual contributions received by a candidate and the expenses of the candidate's campaign—are often the most voluminous. They're important because they can unveil donors who may have questionable relationships with the candidate, or special interest groups with positions and agendas that might cause voters to question or reconsider their support for a candidate. They reveal the sources of a candidate's money, from friends and neighbors or from giant foreign corporations that spill millions of gallons of oil into American waters. They are important and they can number in the thousands of pages.

The puckish clerk repeats Alan's answer as if she didn't really understand it the first time, then stares back at the names.

"We're talking nearly twenty years' worth," she says as if this fact might change our minds.

"Yes, we know it's a big request, but we're going to need to see them," he says.

"Well, before I can even look at this, you're going to have to fill out this form," she shoots back. "And then I'm going to have to talk to my supervisor."

As she shoves the lengthy, and mostly useless, request form into Alan's chest, her voice becomes even more agitated and strained. She tells us that we can't just walk into her office and ask for something that might take her all day to find. After all, she says, she has work to do. And even if our request is approved by higher powers, don't we know that she'd have to find a dolly to haul it all out here?

I manage to just keep my mouth shut this time, but Alan can't. "Isn't *this* your job?" he asks as he waves his hand in a circular motion in front of her face. "Isn't helping people who need public records what you do? I mean, we'll be glad to help you roll that dolly right on out here."

I choke on the mouthful of water I've just sipped in my attempt to keep from laughing. The lack of air coupled with the flames shooting from our clerk's eyes keeps me in check. Everyone has met someone like her. She's one of those people who, out of a sense of entitlement and stubbornness, insists on driving in the left lane without passing, bottle-necking traffic because she can and always pretending she doesn't see you. She's the person in front of you at the Subway sandwich shop who painstakingly orders every possible extra and every possible condiment on her foot-long, all while quizzing the sandwich maker about the ca-loric intake of each one, oblivious to the ten people waiting behind her. Yet question her actions or inconvenience her in any way and she will cut you into bite-size morsels and chew you up.

Difficult people are a big part of opposition research. Unhelpful government workers with an automatic "no" reflex are very common. Time and again, they stand in your path: people determined to avoid doing any work by thwarting your very best efforts. You enter the re-cords office, the workers are seated at their terminals, perhaps eating pasta salad from a Tupperware container or talking on the phone to a blabby family member, and no one looks up. "Excuse me," you say, and finally one person, likely the most recent hire, grudgingly makes eye contact. You tell her what you're looking for. She says you'll have to officially request that information. You'll have to *fill out the form*. You say OK.

She rises slowly from her desk and shuffles to the counter. When she sees what you want she says, "That's in the archives." She lets you think about this. Maybe you'll say, "Oh, OK, sorry," and leave. When you don't leave, when you say nothing but don't move, she adds, "It would have to be retrieved," as if your request is still, at this point, contingent on some as-yet unproven theory, the implication being that this would be a very big deal. You say, "OK, retrieve it." She asks if you're aware that there is a retrieval fee, which can be as much as twenty dollars, plus one dollar per page to copy, and that it could be hundreds of copies, and that the very retrieval process itself could take up to three days. She makes it sound like an impossibly time-consuming and expensive proposition—the public records equivalent of a manned space mission with no guarantee of a successful return to earth. "No problem," you say. She looks at you as if you're evil.

The only way around such difficulties, aside from finding an alternate clerk, is the seemingly useful public access computer. Such terminals have been installed in courthouses across the country, ostensibly for your convenience, but also to lessen the burden on the employees who would otherwise have to help you. Yes, they contain the information you're likely looking to find, but be warned: Trying to operate some of them can result in intense cranial discomfort, trancelike spells, loss of hair, embarrassing crying jags and recurring nightmares. These computers are usually set off by themselves in some corner of the offices that house them, banished from normal functioning society. No matter what you do or how hard you try, you'll likely never understand how to use them and, in the end, the clerk whose time was supposed to be saved by these technomonsters will be forced to come over and help you anyway.

One regret I have through my years of doing research is that I didn't collect all of the instruction sheets that most every clerk's office in the country posts next to each public access computer. No two are exactly alike and each can be as difficult to decipher and as frustrating as a Greek tragedy written in Chinese on the back of a postage stamp.

One of the most confusing and maddening examples was a three-columned sheet filled with an alphabet soup of the codes required to use the computer. At first glance it seemed simple enough. If I'm looking for this . . . just enter this code. Easy! Want to look for tax liens on a piece of property? "The screens that will assist you in this search are VTAS, RXPN, RXPS, or RXDT," reads the sheet. Once I entered one code, more information was required, such as a property parcel number, which more often than not I didn't have. In the rare instance that I did, there was an entire substratum of information that required even more codes. If I managed to successfully drill down into that data, I'd have better prayed that I didn't have to go back because the information I just accessed would evaporate in the blink of a computer screen and I'd have to start the whole process over again. There was little hope of success in this endeavor and few options but to ask the clerk for help. On her fourth trip over, she looked at the terminal and proceeded to tell me that I was operating in the wrong "session."

"Session?" I asked. "What does that even mean?"

She flipped over the instruction sheet and pointed to a sentence that read, "You may view a document at any time, but you must be using the 'A' session and you must be on the RXEN screen."

I just looked at her and then back at the computer. I had absolutely no clue what in the hell she was talking about. Session? How would I know I'm in the wrong session? How did I get in this session? How many sessions are there? What exactly is a session? Forget it. I don't even care. The whole point of the public access computer had been negated. In the end she was forced to move me from my chair and find the information I sought while I peered over her shoulder.

If I were stranded on a deserted island, one of the things I would most like to have is a public access computer and an instruction sheet. It would keep me occupied for years.

Walking into a tax assessor's office in Minnesota one afternoon, I found Alan sitting in front of a computer nearly in tears. It wears on you. The entire system, from filling out forms to paying fees to arguing with rabid government workers, will beat you down, tempt you to just leave empty-handed, force you never to return. But Alan and I do return. We've learned to endure it, to outlast them. To cannibalize a line by Steve Martin from the movie *Planes, Trains & Automobiles*: "I could tolerate any insurance seminar. For days I could sit there and listen to them go on and on with a big smile on my face. They'd say, 'How can you stand it?'" I'd say, 'Cause I've been to courthouses and government offices from Florida to Oregon. I can stand *anything*. The tactics used to frighten you away or deny your right to review public documents are seemingly endless. One common device is to try to scare you with fees. To this day, the ultimate fee-diversion effort was one that came from an Oregon state agency that attempted to charge an estimated $200,000 for a list of fairly easy-to-compile information.

"The agency is, of course, willing to do this," read the e-mail from its communications office. Of course it is. So I'm thinking, "OK, I can drop them a check in the mail for nearly a quarter million dollars or buy, say, a new house with no mortgage, or perhaps join a feed-the-hungry program and send a dollar a day to a starving kid for the next 547.95 years." Tough choices for sure.

The kicker to all this was the last line of the message, which read, "Additionally, can you please tell me how you intend to use these materials?"

My reply very simply pointed out that I had requested similar information in other states and knew it should be a fairly straightforward process with costs that are minimal at best. I appreciated their interest in my intended use of this information, I stated, but since these are public records, that information is not required.

Ten days later, after a few more e-mails and counter-e-mails, I received the information for which I had asked. And the total cost? Nothing. Zero. No charge. Free.

But for every scare tactic or surly jerk in a records office there's often a counterbalance, a supremely nice and helpful person, like the librarian in the special collections section of the University of Utah library. My search for an obscure masters thesis written some twenty-five years earlier by a candidate now running for Congress led me to the librarian, who combed through library records until he found what I was looking for. And while it was being copied, he asked me to sit and talk to him about politics, about voter apathy and about his hopes for the country. Later, I received an e-mail from him that read, "It was really good to meet you. I hope your visit to the University of Utah's library was productive. I enjoyed our conversation. Have a good summer and let me know if you need anything from the library here."

Such niceties, however, are rare and are certainly nowhere to be found at the government office in Missouri. For three days, an odd battle has continued between us and our disgruntled troll. But we are not to be defeated. Try as she might, she has been unable to throw up enough barriers to stop us from our intended mission. She has been unable to convince her supervisor to halt our request for the campaign finance reports we seek. And though the retrieval process has been slow, she is, piece by piece, bringing out the documents we've requested. Watching a hostile civil servant wheeling a dolly stacked with paper is, in a strange way, a rewarding moment.

"Do you think she hates us?" Alan asks.

"Pretty sure," I say. "I mean, look at her."

After three consecutive days of us, she no longer walks with the air of defiance we had witnessed that first afternoon. She only speaks when we have a question. She looks tired, and part of me feels bad that she has lost a battle she was so confident she would win. It's not easy being a government employee. For the most part, the work is tedious and the pay is low. And when two smart-assed strangers walk in and ruin half your week, the job likely seems that much harder.

For a moment I wonder what her life must be like beyond her bureaucratic day job. Does she have a family, and do they find her as troublesome as we do? Does she gripe about the amount of laundry she has to wash, screaming at her children, "I'd have to have a dolly to haul all those clothes to that washing machine!" But then, I think, maybe she's the exact opposite when she's at home. Maybe she's the sweetest, most caring and giving woman in her neighborhood. Maybe people come from miles around just to be in her presence and absorb some of her at-home charm.

"I kind of feel sorry for her," I tell Alan.

"Not me," he snaps back, without looking up from his work.

"Yeah, me either."

It's about thirty minutes to closing when she walks up and tells us that she'll be leaving soon. She assumes since her day is ending, ours is too. For three days we've gone through the reports we need to see and she's likely breathing a little easier because she believes we'll now be leaving for good. She flippantly asks if there will be anything else.

"Just one more thing," says Alan as he slams a heavy stack of reports onto the end of the table in front of her and leans back in his chair. "We're going to need copies of all this. Could ya do that for us?"

9

Alan

Over the years, Michael and I have watched with quiet dismay as a host of transcontinental government employees stand in the way of private citizens seeking copies of public documents. Particularly when it's late in the campaign season, after we've been dealing with bureaucratic hurdles all summer long, we sometimes feel an urge to intervene—to tell people that no matter what they may hear from the clerk who steadfastly refuses to rise from her homey, personal-photo-infested desk, no one can deny them public records.

The desire to assist others who are being rebuffed by imperious minor authority figures developed in me early on, when, as a sixth grader armed with a small spiral notebook known on the playground as "Alan's little black book," I compiled a detailed, running indictment of our teacher, a churlish sociopath. I was inspired to document her transgressions because the other children were helpless to do much other than cry or fantasize about her being kidnapped by aliens and transported to another universe aboard a flying saucer. I needed a more attractive, actionable response.

The little black book was wildly successful as a social networking tool. It was, essentially, a titillating, password-protected blog. Empowered by my role as secret documentarian, I eventually went public with the teacher's most damnable act—the violent swinging, by the arm, of a boy with a severe learning disability. In that case I was moved to act even before the episode made its way into the record.

Following the teacher's shocking display of abuse, as my classmates sat mute at their desks and the targeted boy stared out the window, rubbing his arm, I briefly commiserated with my friend Melanie, who shared my budding sense of impropriety, and the two of us rose from our desks and walked silently to the principal's office, where we delivered the news. The principal listened to our account without a word, and then directed us back to the classroom. A few minutes later she arrived in class and sternly addressed the children, expressing her solidarity with the teacher and chastising us for not being patient with her mood swings, which she said were the result of fluctuations related to "goiter." During this, the teacher sat smugly behind her desk, fiddling with her bra strap under her dress. Authority.

In a sense, Melanie and I had failed, though it's worth noting that the teacher never bothered the slow boy again, nor did we, the two rapscallions, suffer any repercussions. Perhaps it was assumed that while we had been temporarily defused, we still posed something of a threat; we might, after all, tattle to our parents. (We didn't.)

Soon after that, I lost my little black book, the memory of which haunts me to this day. In its era, losing the little black book was the equivalent of misplacing a red-hot opposition research report in a public place. I searched for weeks—on the playground; in the vicinity of the dreaded maypole (where it could have flown from my pocket during the awkward physical movements required by the garish, confusing spectacle); on the verges of the soccer field; in my secret box in the garage; along the creek where I played. It never resurfaced.

Though my program to undermine our classroom's vexing, publicly sponsored ogre through documentation ultimately failed, the concept clearly held promise, and it earned the admiration of my peers while conferring on them a much-needed sense of empowerment. Today, as an adult oppo guy, I feel the same self-righteous zeal when I see citizens being cowed by public employees whose personal power is derived from the mere presence of a countertop.

Occasionally, out of a mixture of pity, camaraderie and mischief, Michael and I have offered unsolicited private instructions to those we've observed in such situations. At some point, likely as we were driving from one stone-faced records edifice to another, it occurred to us that we could provide a handy guide for dislodging impervious government employees, thereby freeing the exchange of telling documentation. Ideally, we would provide our pointers on a laminated sheet that would be required by law to be posted in every records repository across the land. Because the world is not ideal, we offer them here.

Whomever you come up against, it's important to recognize that there are special considerations for each city and each region. Difficult clerks may seem interchangeable, but in fact they are site-specific, bringing their own regional culture and the vagaries of personal identity to the counter. Obviously, the hope is that you will arrive at that counter or window, state your request, and receive your documents without controversy. To increase the chances of that happening, we advise engaging them on their own terms, at least at the outset. It may be useful to talk country in rural areas, or no-nonsense in Chicago, or to present yourself as a charming curiosity, which, in our case, may mean laying on the Southern charm in Idaho. It is also sometimes useful to flirt with the person, whether male or female, depending on your gut feeling. Some of the tactics summarized below require practice, and are advisable only for the advanced practitioner, but even a novice can master most of them quickly.

1.   Arrive at the records repository first thing in the morning, when clerical enthusiasm is highest; or just before or after lunch; or just before closing time, when there is a greater sense of clerical urgency.

The utility of the time threat was revealed to me during a research project in California, where a lunchtime stroll through the lovely redwoods of the Muir Woods park resulted in my getting lost, after which I was late arriving at the county's government center, as the clock was approaching 5:00 PM. I was initially embarrassed to be making a significant records request when everyone was preparing to go home, but lo and behold, the records clerk, after an introductory sigh, proceeded to manically gather and copy the majority of the documents in record time. There is nothing like the approach of quitting time to inspire a clock puncher to get the job done. He didn't even take the time to ask me whom I was with.

The next day I arrived promptly at 8:00 AM to complete my task. It was a beautiful morning, with shafts of sunlight falling through the arched skylights of the stunning Frank Lloyd Wright–designed county building, and as I approached the counter, a different clerk greeted me, fresh as a flower. "What a beautiful building," I said, and she agreed. Then I explained my purpose and slid my records request across the counter. She smiled and went to work.

In summary: The clock can be your friend.

2. Be nice, but confident. If you're in a locale where people still maintain a sense of decorum, you may want to start off with something like, "Hello, my name's Eric [or Erica]. Could you tell me how to go about finding the tax history of this piece of property? Is that something I can do on my own?" If you're someplace where being polite is considered antiquated and a sign of weakness, cut to the chase: "I need the tax history for a piece of property and all I have is the owner's name. Think you can help?"

Michael and I have observed that rambling, uncertain citizens with unclear needs are among the chief vexations of government employees consigned to dealing with the public. While posing as one can be useful as a last-ditch diversionary tactic, it's never good to start out that way. Everyone, including the others waiting in line, will be annoyed when someone approaches the counter and announces, tentatively, "I'm not sure exactly what I'm looking for. I was thinking—last night, while watching *Dancing with the Stars*?—that I couldn't remember if my mother's sister-in-law, an older lady who lives in the . . . oh, what's the name of that assisted living place out on the bypass, the one with the fountain out front? I'm having a senior moment myself, ha ha ha . . ."

You do not want to be that guy. Everything that takes place in proximity to him is going to be tedious and counterproductive. Inexperience, even feigned ignorance, can be a plus, but even then it's important to remain focused.

3.   Assume the best, starting out. Smile. Scientists have found that approximately 25 percent of the human population is comprised of assholes; 25 percent, idiots; 25 percent, idiotic assholes; and 25 percent, people who are smart or nice or both. The breakdown is easily observed on any interstate highway. At the outset, assume that clerks are part of the latter group until proven otherwise, and make clear that you are, too. Even if they reveal themselves to be idiotic assholes and you have to fall back on verbal pepper spray, do not make the mistake of assuming a kindred role as a petty nuisance. It will only make things harder, and the people behind you in line will hate you, too. This doesn't mean you can't be forceful (see item number 6, below).

4.   Incentivize. Show gratitude for any help the employee provides. Try to make the process work efficiently so that everyone can move on to other things. Don't get too friendly, though, lest you open the door for them to inquire about your reasons for doing the research, at which point your reticence may spoil the pleasant atmosphere you've just created. Also, they may know the person.

Not all on-the-ground records research takes place in public offices; sometimes it's necessary to inquire at private businesses—always a tricky wicket, in that they are not sub-ject to full public disclosure and have the right to refuse. Still, most of the same rules of interpersonal dynamics apply.

I was once doing research in a newspaper library, a place that is rarely open to the public, but into which I had finagled entry by using the vernacular language of a newspaper reporter—throwing out words like "clip files," "the morgue" (as newspaper archives are known, in-house), etc. The lion's share of archived news stories are available online, through subscription services or at newspaper web-sites, but doing a thorough job sometimes requires going further back in time or through the archives of smaller newspapers than are available through those mechanisms. Such was the case in the small town in South Carolina where I entered the newspaper archives (far preferable to a local library, which may not index its clips) by behaving as a reporter, which had the unintended side effect of opening me to chitchat with actual staff writers, who are by nature and profession a curious bunch. Where did I work? Where had I worked? What was I looking for and why? I was hit with a barrage of meaningful and logical questions, deliv-ered amicably by a perceived peer.

What to do? Michael and I never lie; finding and fur-thering the truth is our guiding light, the very purpose of our mission. We are not above being cagey or creative, but both are tactics that reporters are adept at identifying—and quickly. When the friendly journalist pressed me for answers, I could neither refuse nor tell the whole truth and risk blow-ing my and our campaign's cover. My search itself would be the fodder for a story.

I had, by this point, revealed the newspaper I had once worked for on a daily basis, which prompted the reporter to suggest the names of other reporters whom we might know in common, and as it turned out, one of my former colleagues worked at that very paper. Oh, hey! I had answered truthfully right up to the point that I realized I was in a conversational box canyon, so I closed my notebook, looked the reporter in the eye and said, "I'm working on my own now, and I can't really talk about the story. But if I find anything, I promise to share it with you." She was satisfied, and in fact the campaign did share my findings with her, but it was a near-miss just the same.

5.   If the person in charge attempts to stifle you, perhaps by speaking in an unknown tongue, or implying that what you're asking for is unreasonable, stand quietly and say nothing. Let them work through the possibilities. If necessary, act stupid. You'd be surprised how easy and fun this can be, once you overcome having been trained to pretend you know things when you don't. Look down at your shoes and say, "I don't understand" at least twice. Scratch your head, even.

Sometimes Michael and I really don't know; we've been given a specific assignment, such as to get copies of a lawsuit, and we have no idea who, ultimately, wants the information or why. But more often we merely imply that we're dumb, when doing so will play on the sympathies of a clerk who holds the power to make our job far more difficult, perhaps by imposing long wait times for document request reviews and the like. We might start out by saying, "Is it possible to find out whether another person pays his taxes?" Of course, we know it is, but are also aware (based on office atmospherics) that immediately launching into a request for a well-known candidate's tax history could cause resistance. For the moment, we're just guys who have no idea how anything works, who are at the mercy of strangers, who need help.

So, after we ask if it's possible to get a person's tax history, the clerk will say, "Sure, you can do that. You just give me the name and I can call it up." Then he or she smiles as one might smile at a slow child, and says, "What's the name?" You blurt out the well-known candidate's name; the clerk looks up at you; you retain the blank, helpless look. Everyone knows the clerk has been trapped, and can't refuse or even complicate the request now.

6.   Try not to be a nuisance—right up to the point when it becomes apparent that anything you say or do is considered a nuisance. When that happens, go ahead and become a serious nuisance. Run with it. Ask endless questions. Make clear that you have all the time in the world. But again, be careful never to completely cross the line into assholedom. Allow them to hate you—hate is corrosive, and wears them down—but let the decision to hate be theirs alone. You can influence the timing, and you should, in subtle ways. If they hate you too soon, they may manage to gain an edge on you.

In a New Jersey township where I've done oppo numerous times over the course of many years, I have become acquainted with two archetypal public employees. One was a supremely nice woman who quickly figured out what I was up to when I asked for a slate of candidate's voting records. She actually seemed to appreciate what I was doing. She was charged with maintaining public voting records, after all, and no doubt felt that asking whether candidates voted themselves was a valid question.

Then there was the clerk in the criminal records division across town who invariably reacted with disgust over whatever request I made, no matter how routine. After appearing at their counters for several years in a row, both women began to recognize me, but for the criminal records czar, familiarity had bred contempt—beyond, even, that she routinely mustered for anyone who walked in the door. It was written all over her face. Sometimes, just to fulfill her need to hate me, I would ask her to check the criminal record of a candidate, and after she returned to say, in a borderline vicious tone, "*No*, there's nothing in their name," I would depart, walk down the hall and then pause and return with another request, sometimes for a name I'd made up; once I even used my own. "Nothing on Alan Huffman? OK, thanks! Have a nice day!" The truth is each time I arrive in town I look forward to seeing both of these public servants, for different reasons.

7.   If nothing you do dislodges them, mention the open records law, making sure to use the correct title, which varies from state to state. Even if the clerk is being adversarial, use a thoughtful tone, as in, "Oh, is this not a public record?" as if you don't know for sure but you assume they do. If that doesn't work, say simply, "I know this is a public record."

Each state has an open records law, though they vary to some degree. In one race, a records clerk refused to give me a copy of a tax lien filed against a candidate. "Is that not a public record?" I asked.

"It is," she said, "But it contains some information that is protected by privacy laws."

"Well, then," I said. "How does that work? It's a public record, but it can't be viewed by the public?"

She stared at her computer screen. "I can read the parts to you that aren't private," she said.

"OK," I said. I ended up taking notes as she read to me. It was a little unnerving when the campaign used the information in an ad, knowing that I couldn't produce copies of the document, but I knew where to send anyone who might challenge the claim.

8.   If you encounter a particularly skillful opponent and he or she gets the best of you, owing to their vast insider

knowledge of bureaucratic operations and the ability to frighten children *too much* on Halloween, move on to another task in another agency office, then return during lunch when someone else is at the window. The chances are they can't stand that person, either.

9.   Admittedly, there are times when you may want to throw your laminated sheet to the side and say, "Listen, this isn't the CIA and I don't have time to stand here while you figure out ways *not* to do what you're paid to do. So here's a novel idea—*just do it!*" Michael loves this option, though I should point out that he uses it judiciously. Before you reach this point of no return, you should make every effort to exhaust all the possibilities and avoid a showdown, particularly in a building with guards, and when drawing too much attention to your request will ensure that someone will alert the politician, who will immediately start doing damage control.

10.   When all else fails, ask to see the person's supervisor. Bonus points: Know the supervisor's name beforehand. You can find it on the office website or by scanning the room for photographs, employee-of-the-month awards or desk nameplates. Forcing the supervisor into play means bad internecine publicity; it indicates failure on the clerk's part.

If, by chance, you're fortunate enough to encounter a particularly helpful public servant, call back later, ask for the supervisor and tell them what a gem of an employee he or she has working for them. Few people ever do that, and they should.

10

Michael

The last time I had the crap kicked out of me was in college. I don't remember exactly what precipitated the altercation that night, but I do recall being a tad drunk outside a convenience store, holding a bag full of greasy potato logs and shoving a finger in the guy's face. The only difference between then and right now is that I'm not drunk, I don't have any logs and I'm standing inside a county courthouse.

It's midsummer and I've been trying for a month to get my hands on one court file. I've had enough. Government offices, whether local, state or federal, can be difficult to navigate. If you're lucky you can just walk in and ask for the information. In other cases you have to fill out forms and come back a day or two later. In some instances you have to write letters, officially requesting the information under the state and federal open records laws that allow for its release. Sometimes, however, no matter what route you take, nothing works.

The file I'm seeking, which I've been told holds information about an infidelity committed by the candidate we're researching, is supposed to be stored in the county clerk's office along with every other court file. The case has long since been resolved, but this particular file has been "checked out" by the attorney who handled it. Why? Because he wants to protect his client from the damage it could cause.

Over the past four weeks I've called and sent letters to no avail. The clerks don't know when the file will be returned and have so far not been inclined to retrieve it themselves. Even my phone calls to the attorney's office have proved fruitless. So, on this morning, I tell Alan I have no option but to drive to the courthouse and confront the bureaucracy in person.

"I'm going to spend an entire day on this bullshit," I grumble.

"Remember to smile," Alan says as I walk out the door.

It's a painstaking drive down rural highways and one-lane back roads to the small-town courthouse that is the source of my irritation. When I enter the clerk's office, I introduce myself as the guy who's been phoning and writing about the file that's not there.

"Still hasn't been returned," one of the clerk's says quickly.

"Tell me," I say. "If it *were* here, where would it be?"

She leads me back to a records room, points at rows and rows of shelves crammed with folders stuffed with legal papers, and tells me that what I'm seeking would be there, if it were there, which it's not. She asks if I need the case number to search for the missing document. I already have it, I tell her, and she leaves. I thumb through the files one by one in sequence until I get to the spot where it should be. There, in its place, is a small note card indicating that, indeed, the candidate's attorney removed the file some months earlier. I take it out, walk back to the clerk and set it in front of her.

"Exactly how long can someone 'hijack' a court file?" I ask. "I mean, it's county property, right? Do you have any interest in getting it back?"

The clerk starts to formulate a response when she looks over my shoulder through the door of an adjacent courtroom, points and says, "Ask him. He's the one who has it."

There, standing among a roomful of court personnel wrapping up some hearing, is an average-looking man in a dark suit packing up his briefcase.

"That's *this* guy?" I ask with my finger on the name scrawled on the note card. "That's the attorney?" She nods.

The object of my ire is preparing to leave, or so he thinks.

Housed directly behind the forehead of every human are chunks of brain called the frontal lobes. These lobes are chock-full of dopamine-sensitive neurons that help control our emotions. Their functions, according to medical books, are to recognize future consequences resulting from current actions, to choose between good and bad conduct and to override and suppress unacceptable social responses. In humans, the frontal lobes reach full development in our twenties as we reach the cognitive maturity associated with adulthood. I can only assume, however, that sometimes, on some days, the frontal lobes simply decide to take a snooze.

Our conversation begins nicely enough. I introduce myself to the attorney, describe my problem and ask if I might see the court file that he possesses. He says nothing for several moments, goes back to his briefcase and then asks, "Why do you want it?"

My frontal lobes are apparently sound asleep. "First, it's none of your business why I want it. Second, it's not your file to keep. Third, as far as I'm concerned, you stole it," I tell him.

The others in the courtroom, including the judge, are now listening. The rage I'm directing at this attorney is surprisingly fulfilling after a month of being stonewalled. He tells me he's not sure he even has the file. I show him the card with his name on it and he just smiles. This guy is a classic dick and all I want to do is keep going. I also realize that I'm in unfamiliar territory and, on one level, I understand the perils that can arise from starting trouble in a place where you know no one.

In the movie *Chinatown* there's a scene in which Jack Nicholson's character, Jake Gittes, a private detective, is tailing a man on behalf of his supposed wife, to see if he is having an affair, not knowing that he's been tricked. At one point in his investigation, which includes researching land and water rights records in the county courthouse, Gittes realizes that he may be bumping up against something bigger than one man's infidelity—something that involves political corruption, the swindling of farmers and a conspiracy to control the flow of water to the thirsty, growing city of Los Angeles. If there were any doubt about it, his suspicions are confirmed when a thug slices his nose with a knife for being "a very nosy kitty."

Neither Alan nor I had ever been subjected to physical assault, but we've received our share of threats, and we take note of episodes involving others who encounter trouble on similar quests. You've probably never heard of Ajay Kumar, but he lives in New Delhi, India, and, like me, was just asking questions and digging for the truth. In India, any citizen is entitled to ask for information from any level of government under the nation's Right to Information Act, adopted in 2005. So when Kumar (not to be confused with Ajay Kumar, the world's smallest actor) discovered that private buildings were encroaching on government land under the protection of a local politician, he asked the Municipal Corporation of Delhi why these homes and shops were allowed to be built on property not zoned for private construction. At first he was denied, ignored by the public information officer. But he persisted and took his questions to a higher-level public information officer and then to the federal government's central information commission. Success at last, Kumar must have thought, when the commission ordered the local government and the police to inspect the property about which he had inquired. He must have felt a sense of vindication and pride that he had taken on the powers that be and won a victory, not only for himself, but also for his neighbors and the citizens of his city. He must have believed that the system had worked.

Unfortunately for Kumar, when he returned to the property a few months later, he was savagely attacked and beaten bloody with an iron rod by an angry mob of two dozen people who backed the politician he had crossed.

"Neither the police nor the people helped me," said poor Kumar in a *Time* magazine article.

Miles from home, I wonder who's going to help me if this thing goes south. I don't know how many friends this attorney has or who they are. Maybe the sheriff? Maybe the judge? Here I am, standing in a courtroom, half shouting at a man I've never met before, all because he has a file I want to see. Is it worth it?

"I'll bring it back when I'm ready," he tells me.

It's worth it.

"No, here's what you're going to do." My right index finger is now about two inches in front of his face. "You're going to go to your office, get the file and bring it back to the clerk where it belongs. You don't own it and your client doesn't own it. It belongs to the county. So go get it."

In poker, when players make mistakes because something has upset them emotionally, it's called "being on a tilt." A player becomes so upset that he begins to make poor decisions. A player can sometimes go on a tilt simply because his opponent is obnoxious or rude. And a player on a tilt may begin betting with weaker hands than usual. While it's important to recognize when your opponent is on a tilt, it's even more vital to understand when you may be going on a tilt and figure out how not to let your emotions get the best of you. I'm definitely on a tilt, but it's too late. I've already laid down my bet and called his hand.

The attorney looks away and glances briefly at the judge, who, I'm relieved to see, has a hint of a grin on his face and a look that says, "Hey, don't ask me to help you." It's just me and the attorney—no angry mob. Everyone still in the courtroom knows he's purposely hiding information he is not entitled to keep.

With few options except to continue ignoring me or hit me on the head with an iron rod, he finally agrees to have someone from his office return it and tells me I can get it from the clerk. A few days later I do, and it contains the information I am seeking. Though it was never used in the campaign, it was nonetheless a victory, the payoff for a well-played hand.

Things don't always end that well. Sometimes you meet assholes along the way. But fortunately it's rare for anyone to be killed or beaten in the United States today for merely asking questions, for seeking information to which we are entitled. Whether it stays that way in these volatile political times is anyone's guess.

11

Alan

On May 14, 1993, XXXXXX advised the president that XXXXXX had participated in a meeting during which XXXXXX, XXXXXX and XXXXXX reviewed the XXXXXX of the XXXXXX (relative to the Clean Air Act Amendments of 1990) and concluded that XXXXXX would cause XXXXXX to XXXXXX.

All true statements! It happened during the administration of President George H. W. Bush.

OK, so it's not a verbatim transcript. Michael and I long ago disposed of our copy of the original presidential memo, but such are the kinds of political "bombshells" we find among the files we receive from the Bush Presidential Library in response to our voluminous Freedom of Information Act request. The memos, covering the activities of a former presidential aide we're researching, are so heavily redacted that they contain few complete sentences. Scanning them for anything of value is a dizzying, futile exercise.

The administration's lack of transparency is no surprise, considering the availability of executive privilege, but we've arrived at the presidential library in College Station, Texas, hoping we'll get lucky and catch a glimpse of something substantive regarding a man being considered for an appointment by then-president George W. Bush. The prospective appointee, known affectionately as XXXXXX, had served as an aide to the elder Bush, and our hope is that the staff of the newly opened library is unprepared for the likes of us and might let the archived memos slip through. In fact the staff *is* unprepared, but we end up being denied anyway, passive-aggressively, no doubt as a result of a directive from above.

We're interested in four hundred boxes of files, only a handful of which have been opened for public review, and so we request access to the entire collection, which totals about forty-five hundred pages. After we receive our blacked-out copies, President George W. Bush issues a controversial executive order limiting public access to presidential archives. As a result, Bush also effectively closes his own gubernatorial files, which he had stashed in the presidential library rather than in the state archives, where they would have been available to scholars, journalists and the general public. Though President Barack Obama later rescinded the executive order, and the Texas state archives took the position that the gubernatorial files are state property, subject to the state's open records law, be forewarned: If you visit the presidential library in hopes of learning about the inner workings of the administration of Bush-the-elder as president, or Bush-the-younger as governor, you may want to have a backup plan. Otherwise you could be forced to spend your time chatting with a sweat-stained German tourist, which is what I do while Michael handles the dirty work of upsetting the records clerk.

Before arriving in College Station, we researched XXXXXX in various cities across the Midwest and along the Eastern Seaboard. It's now late in the season, and we've made the last leg of our journey, a seven-hour road trip from Jackson, in my silver roadster. Michael and I figured a road trip would be a nice intermission from the tedium and inconvenience of air travel and cheap rental cars. We'd be just like the two guys on the old *Route 66* TV show who roamed the United States in a drop-top Corvette, searching for adventure, never knowing what might unfold in the next town along the way. Except it didn't really work out that way for us.

Even when there's something to sink your teeth into, presidential appointments are notoriously difficult to derail. Supreme Court Justice Clarence Thomas's confirmation hearings were notably contentious, focusing on allegations that he'd made unwelcome sexual comments to a subordinate attorney, yet he was confirmed anyway. In our case, it was apparent that our research was going nowhere long before we arrived at the presidential library. Even the road trip was a disappointment. The summer sun was blazingly hot with the top down, and because Michael and I are middle-aged guys with thinning hair, we lacked the cinematic appeal of the hunky young *Route 66* guys. Plus, the highway department was in the process of repaving long stretches of I-20, which resulted in tar splatters on my shiny silver fenders, and after many long days together Michael and I were starting to get on each other's nerves. A side effect of trafficking in negative information is that it sometimes rides right alongside us in the car, with the inevitable result that Michael starts intentionally smacking his gum because he knows it annoys me. As we drove across Texas, I could hear his gum smacking over the roar of the highway wind.

Once at the presidential library, we spend several hours going through the indexes, compiling a list of documents we want to review. It's monotonous work, and when it comes time to approach the clerk with our request, I wander off to chat with the *touristischen*, who is dressed in the modern equivalent of lederhosen—maroon pants pulled too high, with fanciful stitching on the back pockets. As he and I discuss the landscape of America, I notice Michael occasionally glaring at me from his station at the counter, where a phalanx of staffers has gathered around the bewildered clerk to engage in familiar document-request sortie. At one point the German, discussing air travel, blurts out the word "Lufthansa!" very loudly, and everyone at the counter looks at us accusingly. The truth, meanwhile, is preparing to run for cover.

Irritation, in and of itself, is not necessarily a bad thing in our line of work. It's one of the tools of our trade. Michael and I are driven by our irritation with mendacity and secrecy, and energized by the displeasure of recalcitrant records clerks. But we have different approaches to using that tool, which sometimes causes the interpersonal dynamics of Huffman & Rejebian to be fraught with peril. In short, we tend to irritate each other. We have managed to achieve a kind of détente, whereby we ignore each other's transgressions in service of the greater goal. But the truth is, like it or not, our differences serve the job well. Michael tends to be more organized and focused, less interested in the extras of whatever political drama we're following than in the key players and supporting actors, with the result that he may miss what to me are interesting and telling asides. I'm more likely to come back with something unexpected, such as when a random, rambling conversation with a retired logger revealed that a powerful congressman had facilitated the lucrative transfer of thousands of acres of national forest land to an old friend. Then again, I sometimes miss key dialogue, and my only takeaway is "Lufthansa!" Our different approaches to doing the work make it less likely we'll miss something.

As in any human intercourse, certain characteristics that are annoying or counterproductive in one application serve other purposes quite well. Petty attention to detail is useful when it results in important documentation; it's bad when it leads to painstaking concealment of the truth. It all comes down to what a person chooses to do with the tools at his disposal, which, fortunately, is something that can also be documented. A redacted document is revealing for what it refuses to say.

Politics is the engine of history, and its documentation provides the only permanent record, which is crucial considering that even on a good day the political world is characterized by barely controlled chaos. What people say and do, as reflected in the record, illustrates their fitness to lead during good times or bad. If, by chance, society should break down, as it did after Katrina, who would you want to lead you through the postapocalyptic landscape? Would it be someone who redacts memos? It would pay to look closely at what your potential leader chose to reveal—or conceal—and what they actually did compared with what they said or didn't say. Would you want your tribe to be led by a mayor who grants municipal contracts to political donors, or a waitress with the audacity to break into a flood-ravaged school and begin preparing meals on an open fire for hundreds of survivors? Would you choose as a leader a person who spent an inordinate amount of time in careful exposition, using buzzwords and entertaining yet unaccountable anecdotes, or someone who spoke honestly and only when he or she had something meaningful to say? Would you want someone who beat up his girlfriend in an airport terminal, or someone who rushed to her aid? Someone who feared public revelation, or was honest and forthright? And how could you tell the difference?

Even after years of researching political misdeeds, Michael and I are amazed by the lengths to which some candidates—on both sides of the political aisle—will go to get elected, and by what they will attempt to conceal or redact, or will publicly say, often in contradiction to the public record or in gross violation of logic. If a candidate has something to hide, it's very risky to try to conceal it, and if what he attempted to conceal is brought to light, how he responds is always telling. The days of closely controlling and containing information are gone. There are a host of carefully calculated institutional barriers, such as dazzle camouflage and time-honored subterfuge, which, like an old, drunk liar of a friend, will never, ever go away, and it does sometimes look like facts are going out of style. But facts have staying power, and sometimes the very act of concealing or attempting to conceal them is its own revelation.

Considering what can often be found in candidates' records, it probably should come as no surprise that some of them attempt to keep the public in the dark. For Michael and me, the worst case of political solipsism was the candidate who was running on a family values platform, which included something he called "empowerment of parents," who nonetheless made personal loans to his own campaign and simultaneously reduced his daughter's child support payments to a mere $22.50 per week. He never mentioned this, of course, but it was there in the public record and he had no way to legally prevent its discovery. Whether the guy rationalized that winning would put him in a better position to support his daughter or was driven by blind, selfish ambition, he had a choice to make regarding his campaign finances. He chose poorly.

I can imagine how this revealing scenario began. The guy was probably behind in his fund-raising efforts and found himself wondering, "Do people not realize how expensive it is to run for office? Do they not understand how much is at stake?" Perhaps it was time for the campaign to send out direct mail and there was already a stack of unpaid bills from printers, the phone company and the local newspaper. As he searched for a means to make up the difference, he realized he had some money of his own that he could loan to his campaign, as candidates often do, though it wasn't much and there was still the matter of the freaking child support. What to do?

"Make the loan," the miniature horned candidate on his shoulder exhorted him, while the tiny winged candidate on his other shoulder gazed out the window. So he made the loan and stole from his daughter. He shirked his responsibility as a father to save his campaign, and unfortunately, it paid off. He was elected. Someone, somewhere, dropped the ball. We didn't hear until later, back at the office, that he had won. It mattered a great deal to us that the wrong guy won, because his offenses were so offensive. Finding the truth can be arduous, or it can be as simple as taking the time to peruse a routine public record. Either way, there's no guarantee anyone will care.

Any candidate can pay lip service to campaign positions, but the underlying question, as he sits in repose under a sunlamp, or spends an evening sipping expensive wine with a lobbyist for a hazardous waste disposal company in a dim Capitol Hill bar, or exchanges an aching glance with an intern who sports one of his own campaign buttons, is what sort of documentable details may be discerned from the incremental decisions he or she has otherwise made—the contracts they've signed off on; the votes they've cast or missed; the political deals, big and small, they've been party to; the telling comments they've made in official memos. It isn't necessary to catch someone in flagrante delicto, though that's always nice, or to find that they've received an outright or even a technically legal bribe. You can find out a great deal of what you need to know through the public record, assuming no one has tampered with or censored it.

This is not to say that a candidate's history of late payment of taxes or his use of a derogatory term in a private meeting precludes him from being a good leader. Everyone makes mistakes. Everyone says things they wish they could take back. Everyone redacts his public life to some degree. As Michael and I probe the recesses of candidates' lives I often wonder what details might be used against me if I were running for office. Promiscuity? Thriftlessness? That episode involving the Dutch guy in the Sahara Desert, the subsequent confrontation with the FBI and my not-entirely-flattering article about counterterrorism efforts for the *Washington Post Magazine*? Does my penchant for blithely sending untold tons of aluminum beer cans to the county landfill, rather than recycling them, undermine my avowed support for environmental causes, despite the fact that I've covered endangered species and once went on a Sierra Club outing involving a sailboat and a group of people who droned incessantly about birdsongs, which compelled me to wander off down the beach to go skinny-dipping in the blue-green waters of the Gulf of Mexico alongside a family of porpoises? What about the time my dog bit a neighbor lady and I afterward told a funny story about it, numerous times, at parties? Could I be portrayed as insensitive, perhaps even a public nuisance? Do such details indicate my unfitness to serve as a political leader? Yes, absolutely they do. That's not the role you want me to play in our postapocalyptic tribe or in the proving ground of everyday life.

What you want from people like Michael and me is the ability to document and discern, to stand in the shadows of the campfire under the bridge and judge the behavior of current or prospective leaders, based on factual evidence. If we see the guy saying something that contradicts what he has been observed to do earlier in the day, we will let you know. Perfidy is like theft or any other criminal behavior: The tribe may be able to make use of it, occasionally, such as during a violent conflict—otherwise, no, and particularly not among the leadership class of a moderately functional civilization.

In his song "New Test Leper," R.E.M. front man Michael Stipe sings, "Judge not lest ye be judged/What a beautiful refrain." And it's true. It is a beautiful refrain. But does that stop us from judging? It most assuredly does not. We all judge. It's how we decide what to do every day, whom to follow, with whom to align ourselves or how to attempt to lead. The politicians we elect will pass and enforce laws governing almost every aspect of our lives, and we'll be judged by our compliance. Considering that, does it not matter what they say and do behind the scenes?

Does it not matter when we uncover how a district attorney dropped or failed to file as many criminal cases as he prosecuted; was plainly subjective in deciding who went to trial, sparing people with whom he was closely associated; had a record of softness—and not in a good way—regarding the prosecution of crimes against women; and, along the way, fought against a proposed facility for mentally ill and chemically dependent men because of its potential impact on residential property values in the area? While this guy was DA, one of every six people tried for murder walked away free after their trials, including, in one case, a man charged with stabbing his cousin seventeen times. According to one editorial in the local paper, the acquittal rate suggested that either more people were getting away with murder in the county or more were being wrongfully accused. Seriously: real guy. That's the kind of stuff we find.

This DA had also reduced the charges for a man who'd shot a teenager with a 12-gauge shotgun for trampling his lawn, which touched off a near riot in the neighborhood. An angry crowd gathered in front of the shooter's house, resulting in the beatings of several people, including a police detective and a TV news crew. Thanks to the DA, the shooter received probation. The DA had also declined to prosecute police officers who had transported two intoxicated Native Americans in the trunk of their squad car, which resulted in injuries.

Would such a person make a good leader? Our conclusion was that he most assuredly would not, unless it could be demonstrated that society would benefit from letting well-connected rapists go free and ignoring men who sought treatment for clinically sanctioned problems too close to our homes. At the very least the DA appears to be a documented asshole.

The same goes for the candidate we researched who claimed to be a proponent of campaign finance reform yet championed Tom DeLay, the Texas pest exterminator who later resigned from Congress over alleged violations of campaign laws and money laundering, as well as disgraced lobbyist (and that's saying something) Jack Abramoff, who pled guilty to three felonies related to the defrauding of Native American tribes and corrupting public officials. What sort of campaign finance reform would a candidate who admires such men have in mind, do you think? This same guy also claimed to be against the expansion of government regulation, yet authored legislation that did more than any previous law to enable the government to infringe on personal privacy. And he publicly railed against gambling while taking money from the gaming industry. Who, we might ask, would such a candidate represent?

Then there was our opposing candidate in Ohio, who publicly stated his opposition to abortion in all forms, including emergency contraception (the so-called morning-after pill), who was also against state-sponsored gambling and who supported increased accountability of elections practices—yet who owned stock in companies that produced the morning-after pill, slot machines and voting machines. How might such a candidate be expected to represent his constituency, and to reasonably adhere to his stated personal convictions? What might his actual position be on growing sales of morning-after pills? What company would likely be his preferred source for voting machines, and how might he respond to claims that the machines were faulty, and that therefore the election itself had been thrown into doubt?

The annoyance Michael and I feel over redacted or otherwise hidden truths isn't confined to our opposition research, and it's not merely the result of pathological dissatisfaction. Curiosity is one of the tools of the trade—curiosity about what lies behind the black bar covering the memo text, under the dazzle camouflage, even beneath the ruins of an old farmhouse far out in the country. Such is our love of uncovering hidden truth that we are attracted to any sort of site disturbance, whether it is a political controversy or an archaeological dig. In his spare time, Michael is an avid relic hunter, probing historical ground with a fancy metal detector. He's not the guy searching for lost wedding rings on the beach; he's on a quest to discover clues from the past that illuminate life in any time.

Toward that aim he has spent countless hours probing the ground at my house in rural Mississippi, where he located a Union army camp from the Civil War. He's uncovered a small museum's worth of artifacts from just beneath the surface. Like disjointed, quivering memories, they are clues to the tumultuous past, to lost moments and lost lives: bullets, buttons, buckles, rings and other arcane detritus. Occasionally, he finds items that are not always readily identifiable, such as a lead weight dropped from the hem of a woman's hoopskirt, but in other cases he finds artifacts that are oddly telling, such as a minié ball bullet carved into the shape of a tiny penis, evidence of the sorts of pastimes the soldiers engaged in around the campfire.

Seeing how dedicated he was to exploring the campsite, I have occasionally surreptitiously buried curious metal objects in the area, such as a commemorative coin from the Indy 500, for him to locate, unearth and puzzle over.

"I can't figure out what this is, but it was in the camp," he once said, holding up a large, dirt-encrusted ball of foil that I'd fashioned from Hershey's Kisses wrappers. Then, after examining it more closely, he tossed it at me and said, "Very funny."

Michael's love of history, and of excavating its evidence, are the common denominator of his personal and professional endeavors, and we're alike in that regard. It's all about the process of discovery. The excavation may turn out to be a waste of time, but the point is to get beneath the obscuring surface of things.

Sometimes a single clue brings everything else into sharper focus. During a research project in Kansas City, we happened on two meaningful revelations, one involving a steamboat that sank in the Missouri

River in 1856 and another regarding the sources of campaign funding of an affable-seeming candidate for Congress. The steamboat, the *Arabia*, had struck a snag and gone down in the river with two hundred tons of cargo and was eventually buried under forty feet of silt. The wreckage was excavated in the late eighties, revealing a remarkable archive of unexpurgated facts about life on the American frontier.

On its maiden voyage the boat had transported U.S. soldiers into the Western territories, including what is now the state of Kansas, to subdue Native Americans who were, not surprisingly, hostile. During a later excursion a load of rifles aboard the boat had been seized by the authorities, ostensibly because they were destined for sale to the Indians. The *Arabia* also carried guns for combatants in "Bleeding Kansas," the setting for a proxy war between proslavery and abolitionist settlers of the old American West. In short, the *Arabia*'s history and its cargo were freighted. It wasn't all about beaver hats and calico.

The message of the *Arabia* museum, which we visited over that weekend, is that settlers needed all sorts of very specific things to conquer a continent, and that the American frontier was at once about attacking and abetting those settlers' avowed enemies. Back in the 1850s, some businessman on the frontier, who perhaps railed against the Indians in the local saloon, was secretly involved in selling them guns. Today, his self-serving counterparts are the mercenary businessmen who sell arms to rogue governments overseas, or move their factories to countries with cheaper wages, taking with them hundreds of thousands of American jobs.

Translated for the contemporary immigration debate, which formed the central issue of the opponent's congressional campaign, the inconsistencies of the frontier gun trade were akin to the inconsistencies of hassling illegal aliens while offering them low-paying jobs, and randomly enforcing laws prohibiting employers from hiring them. Though the Kansas candidate presented what appeared to be a thoughtful position on curbing illegal immigration, hidden from view we found what appeared to be darker motivations, judging from some of his sources of funding. He was attractive on the surface, with his careful mannerisms and telegenic good looks, and had, before our arrival, benefitted from a general lack of media curiosity. He was, as they say, all-American looking, though that is a misnomer; he looked nothing like a Native American, having descended from some European line. Then, buried beneath, we found an ugly truth: He had received significant funding from a notoriously racist group. It was there, in the public record.

Campaigns in which all the candidates are black or in which all of the candidates are white tend to respond differently to racial issues than do campaigns in which the slate of candidates is mixed. Race is one of those issues that plays differently from one place to another, but relying on or even accepting the support of a racist group is damaging to a mainstream campaign anywhere nowadays. American history is rife with examples of powerful individuals and groups rolling over the weak, but few people are comfortable admitting they're doing it. When you find a guy running for Congress who gets major funding from an organization that subscribes to the theory that blacks are genetically inferior to whites, you've found a potentially damaging clue.

Michael and I are always excited to point the finger at racists, even if we're sometimes mistakenly swept up in that wide net for the simple reason that we're white guys from below the Mason-Dixon line. We were pleased, therefore, to discover that the Kansas candidate was also linked to the leader of a radical group that denigrated the region's growing Latino population. Even more exciting was that the candidate himself had written that apartheid could be justified in the name of political stability. The candidate's words had not previously been publicized, yet they provided evidence of the kind of intolerance once reserved for hate-mongering groups such as the white Citizens Council in the civil rights–era South.

Perhaps if this had been the 1940s, finding a link between a white candidate and a racially polarizing group would not have been the campaign's death knell. In this case the guy got slammed. Losing didn't prevent him from becoming an outspoken leader of the anti-immigration movement, or from becoming a popular guest of such cable TV hosts as Glenn Beck, however. He managed to make a name for himself, though for our purposes here, he's just another XXXXXX. We aren't here to name names, and not only because we forget them or because someone could be hurt or because many of them are significant only for a while. We, too, have our confidences. Objective and independent though we must be, our research reports are, aside from the public records they cite, confidential, and they become the property of the campaigns for which we work.

No one gives you everything. Michael and I are on a long-running search for facts, but we don't hold ourselves out as the absolute, ultimate sources of truth. We find things. We pass our findings along. They make their way to you. It's all a matter of how much information gets transferred. There are times when redacting is called for. For example, you don't need to see the bloodied body of the murder victim. The WikiLeaks release of documents and videos—generally a laudable effort to make government more transparent—could also endanger American troops. So who, ultimately, should get to draw the line?

In the case of XXXXXX, our presidential appointee, he doesn't appear to be evil—we never see him with the whips and chains—but the truth of his fitness to serve has been summarily concealed. In this manner, liars, scoundrels and obfuscators on both sides occasionally prevail.

XXXXXX would eventually be confirmed, without ever being fully scrutinized, despite our best efforts. No one will ever know, for sure, whether he was the right choice for the position.

12

Michael

In between campaigns, during a busy summer of research, I'm able to take a short retreat to the mountains of Colorado. There, in a wood-framed watering hole in a tiny mining town, I meet Paul. He's preparing to put back a shot of tequila when I introduce myself and ask him how he's doing.

"Well," he says, "I've got a morphine suppository up my ass and I'm doing great."

I like him immediately, and even more so when he tells me that he enjoys a pastime of blasting bowling balls into the sides of mountains from a cannon he built himself. So the following day, I meet Paul next to a mountain as he prepares a demonstration involving sixteen pounds of round hardened plastic, gunpowder and a homemade howitzer.

Dressed in a bowling shirt and a shiny helmet with a steel spike protruding from the top, he shouts a warning from an electronic megaphone to any errant hikers who might have unwittingly wandered downrange of his mortar. Then, with a laugh, he ignites the weapon. As the bowling ball gains altitude, traveling at least a half mile into the air, Paul looks over and shouts, "Listen when it starts coming down because those finger holes will catch the wind and that ball will begin to whistle." Sure enough, it does. And the awe I felt just moments before turns to nervousness and mild panic as the sixteen pounder begins a high-pitched descent in a direction that seems precariously close to me and the other onlookers who've gathered for the show. How do you escape the path of a screaming bowling ball hurtling from the heavens when you have no idea where it's going to land? In the end, you just watch it as it grows larger and larger and hope it doesn't make its final resting place in your head.

It occurs to me, a few days later when I'm back researching one of our own candidates, that political campaigns can be a lot like dodging bowling balls. You never know who is out there, gunning for you, armed with what, or from which direction the attack will come. Further complicating matters, the campaign managers often don't know their own candidates, and sometimes it's hard to tell where the candidates themselves are coming from.

When hired for what's called "self-research," Alan and I have a responsibility to examine our candidates as energetically as we do their opponents, which is crucial, yet perilous. We've researched our share of candidates who were not born leaders, and who resented our finding information about them despite the fact that the other side would likely discover the same things. Candidates have even gone so far as to actually ask us whose side we're on.

One sitting congressman got quite miffed at Alan for discovering that he was in default on his property taxes, and had previously paid them late on numerous occasions. Alan thought he'd want to know that not only did the records reflect several late payments, but that he was late *now*, as in: Maybe you should go pay your taxes. Yet the congressman reacted as if Alan had somehow been responsible for the oversight. No matter what they say, candidates often don't know what's in their own record, and sometimes don't want to, with potentially disastrous results.

Our relationships with just about everyone involved in a campaign, whether it is a pollster, a campaign manager or a candidate, are brief, lasting only as long as the campaign and beginning again when a new season starts. Within a campaign, we're privy to confidential information, but as free agents we're not precisely part of the internal pecking order. The result is that we're sometimes seen as a potential threat, or at best a necessary evil or a killjoy; all that seems to matter to the candidate is our friendly fire. On the flip side, some see us as confidantes—safe, because we're outsiders.

Political campaign staffers are often an itinerant bunch, landing in states and on races with which they are largely unfamiliar. On one race in Florida, the newly arrived campaign manager probably wished he'd landed anywhere else.

Alan and I had worked with him in past elections. He knew his business and knew the components that make up an effective campaign. He needed a poll done quickly to gauge the landscape and to see where the candidates stood in this upcoming race for Congress. But before he could do his poll, he needed research on his own candidate to assess his strengths and weaknesses. So he called us.

As far as we knew, at the time we talked, we'd already been hired. Our proposal had been approved and partial payment for our services was forthcoming, we'd been told. All we needed to do now was talk with the candidate about "campaign 101 stuff," as our campaign manager described it, and get to work. No problem, we'd done it many times before. Just a chat about the basics.

"Why in the hell do I need to hire *you*?" The tone of the first question from our congressional hopeful's mouth took me aback for a moment. "What could you possibly tell me about myself that I don't already know?" he asked, with surprising rancor. "I'm not sure why we're even having this discussion."

This didn't sound like it was going to be a simple introductory course in political research, as predicted, but I was stuck in a position where all I could do was forge ahead. First, I told him, we needed to conduct what's called "self-research," so that we know where he might be most vulnerable. Second, although he might very well be familiar with every detail in his own background, the campaign was not, and needed this information to be able to conduct a poll. Third, the research we do would enable him to better prepare for attacks from his opponent. And finally, I said, "You can rest assured that your opponent is already gathering this same information about you, and he'll use it to his benefit if he can."

I explained to him the research process, how we go about collecting and piecing together information from courthouses, newsclips, state and federal agencies, databases and even acquaintances, when possible and permissible. I told him that we usually begin by interviewing the candidate for background information, which was one reason I'd called today.

This guy was having none of it. His political resume consisted of a stint as mayor of a small city and he honestly seemed to believe he knew what was best for this race. As hard as I tried, I was just not able to convince him that running for mayor and seeking a seat in the U.S. House of Representatives are two different animals. It's the difference between a hornet and an elephant: One can sting you. The other can just stomp you to death.

"You guys are all the same," he said after I finished my brief tutorial.

"I'm not sure I follow you," I replied.

"You political guys, you're all the same. You're just in it for the money."

This wasn't what I had expected, and I didn't even know how to respond, so I didn't. My silence, unfortunately, inspired him to continue.

"I mean, you come into these campaigns and you try to sell us these things we don't need. You see a big pot of money and you want to make sure you get a piece."

All I was trying to do, I told him, was show him the importance of research, as I was asked to do by his campaign manager. In all the years we've worked with campaigns, this was the first time that a candidate had launched into such a bitter tirade. His constant reiteration that there was nothing noteworthy in his background with which he was not already familiar was too much. My first thought was, "What *does* this guy have to hide?"

Our work encompasses admirable candidates, unlikable candidates, simply strange candidates and candidates who lack the potential negatives that we typically dote on. We always look hard, because the worst thing we can do is to overlook something—including something the candidate already knows—that could be used against him. The second worst thing is taking the candidate's word that he's told you everything you need to know and that further research is not necessary. We learned that lesson the hard way some years ago when a candidate running for Congress in Missouri was adamant that he regularly voted in all elections and had never missed casting a ballot since registering to vote. It's not that candidates lie about this stuff; it's that sometimes they just don't remember or don't really know. So we believed him, only checking the votes he had cast in primary and general elections.

Unfortunately, his opponent discovered that he had not voted in a considerable number of local elections and publicly blasted him for his absences. After all, the opponent asked, why should voters give a candidate their vote when he doesn't even make the effort to vote himself?

Needless to say, the campaign was not happy. We took full responsibility for the screwup, the only other option being to say, "But the candidate *told us* he voted." That was never going to fly.

Sometimes we get close to campaign staffers or to the candidate; sometimes we merely do our work, turn it over to them and move on. But for the most part, many of our own candidates seem to feel that the only certifiable difference between us and their worst enemy lies in who gets our report. And, to some extent, that's true.

Our main goal is to make sure our candidates are prepared, to outline, highlight and summarize every salient fact about their life and place it in a political context. Supplementing those points with warnings that "these are the issues you'll be hit with" at least gives the candidate and the campaign time to pause and consider their responses. But sometimes, even when candidates know all there is to know, when they've planned for every contingency, when they think they're ready for what's coming, they still find themselves running side to side in a hail of bowling balls.

During a race in the Midwest, our candidate was getting assailed in TV ads because he had voted for a billion dollars in tax increases in a previous elective office, had a poor attendance record in that office and was involved in some questionable personal business dealings. It had all been there in our report, laid out bullet point by bullet point. It had "be ready" written all over it. Yet for whatever reason, the candidate's primary response was to ask his opponent if he would kindly pull his TV spots and stop the negative campaigning, or conversely, to tell the "full story" behind the tax votes. Of course that wasn't going to happen. First, the ads were factual. Second, they were working. And third, such ads are precisely meant never to tell the full story. They are intended to tell the part of the story that makes the recipient of the attack look like a scumbag.

So our candidate crawled under a desk as the warheads fell and tried his best to weather the attack. With more money in the bank, his opponent was able to buy more airtime and keep the attacks coming. At one point during the campaign, when a political colleague died in office unexpectedly, he hopefully asked his opponent for a cease-fire. Briefly suspending campaign ads during such tragedies is not uncommon and is intended as a show of respect. So our candidate pulled his spots, but his opponent refused to honor the temporary armistice. The assault continued until our candidate was simply bombed into oblivion.

If there is one type of candidate who possibly has it worse than others when it comes to politically accursed backgrounds, it must be judges running for other offices, especially appellate judges or state Supreme Court justices—judges whose job it is to affirm or reverse the decisions of lower court judges. We almost feel sorry for them when they're our candidates because we know that the research is going to almost always turn up the things that make political opponents drool. It's even worse when our candidate is a genuinely honorable person who is only doing his judicial duty.

Portraying your opponent as soft on crime is a powerful weapon, more so when you have the facts to back it up. In this case, our assignment was to dig through the hundreds of opinions of an appeals court judge now running for Congress, looking for those that could cause him the most trouble. Our report to his campaign highlighted more than a handful, including a particularly disturbing case in which he rendered the lone dissenting opinion when it came to his court on appeal. It had trouble plastered all over it.

The offender was a first-grade teacher. His victim was his eight-year-old student. The girl had testified at trial that he would take her to his car and that he would "touch her private parts." He took the girl to a restaurant for dinner, then took her to the bathroom where he unzipped his pants, exposed himself and placed his "private part" between her legs and pressed it against her vagina for twenty minutes.

The offender was convicted of aggravated sexual assault of a child under fourteen and sentenced to twenty-five years in prison. He argued on appeal that the evidence was legally insufficient to establish the element of "penetration with his sexual organ." Two judges affirmed the trial court's judgment. Our candidate disagreed, saying that the state failed to prove he'd penetrated the girl's vagina. Our candidate wrote that there was no evidence to show contact into an area of the body not usually exposed to view, even in nakedness, as the state had alleged in the indictment. From a judge's perspective it wasn't a particularly noteworthy opinion. For a political candidate, it was pretty bad.

The campaign knew that this and other cases could be used negatively against him in the upcoming race, and we knew that he was simply rendering opinions based on his interpretation of the law. In a tight race, such information would likely have been used like a baseball bat by the judge's opponent. But in a heavily partisan district like this one, the race wasn't all that close and our candidate was spared any negative onslaught. At least he was ready.

In the days before the demise of newspapers, Alan and I had the fortune to work in a two-newspaper town. As reporters for the morning publication, the constant threat of being beaten on a story by our counterparts at the afternoon paper kept us tight, vigilant and wary. And, of course, we were always a little worried about the possibility of our editors calling us to their desks to chastise us if we were second on an important news piece. The only comfort was the knowledge that the afternoon reporters always faced the same threat. It was great competition and produced better newspapers for our readers. Opposition research is very similar, the main difference being that we don't really know our competition. We never see them. But we are acutely aware that they're out there, somewhere, always trying to gain the upper hand.

"Someone was just here asking for that same information," a courthouse clerk in a remote town in Kentucky told me one summer afternoon of research. Like a character in an Alfred Hitchcock movie, my first instinct was to slowly peer back over my shoulder, half expecting to see a nondescript man in a dark suit standing in the corner holding a newspaper just below his eyes. Instead, there was only a short, scruffy fellow donning a John Deere cap, waiting impatiently to pay some traffic tickets.

Later, sitting in a records room with twenty strangers, I found myself periodically pulling away from the stack of documents I was reviewing to scan the room, attempting to determine whether the guy in the blue shirt and khaki slacks or the girl in the white dress with the pink cardigan around her neck was poring through the same stack of documents, discovering some tidbit of information that I hadn't come across. One looked up at me briefly, smiled and went back to work. Was that her?

I ordered dinner in the hotel dining room that night, subtly checking each table for the same people from the records room, or someone else who'd ordered the same meal I was having, surmising, with no basis in fact, that all political researchers must eat shrimp pasta with a beer. But then I reminded myself that Republican researchers more likely opt for the filet mignon and a ten-dollar glass of red wine. So I looked for that.

Even on the plane ride home, I inconspicuously moved my eyes to the person sitting in the cramped seat next to me to see what he was reading. Maybe that person was doing the same thing to me, which is why it's always a good idea to stick to the in-flight magazine.

I talked with my candidate and the campaign manager and informed them that someone else had been asking questions and collecting material. "Who were they? Who were they with? What were they looking for?" they asked. In most every case, they become a little freaked out that this "person" even exists.

Sometimes we're able to determine what they were searching for and what they received. Sometimes we aren't. In one instance, we actually filed an open records request seeking all of the open records requests that had been filed in the previous few months. They didn't really tell us anything we didn't already know in terms of factual information, but they did give us an idea of where the opposing campaign might be headed in terms of attacks, and the things about which they were most concerned.

Conversely, our own information requests have sometimes been revealed. During an Arkansas race, a local newspaper reporter responded to claims by the opponent that our research had been "unethical" by filing an open records request for *our* open records requests. The opponent had charged that our candidate used proprietary insurance records to obtain information about health violations at the opponent's restaurant. What the reporter found was that those so-called proprietary records had been public, provided to us by the state health department, so there was no impropriety. Still, the opponent managed to inject me, identified as "a paid researcher," into the campaign.

In another race, our candidate filed suit against the opponent—an incumbent public prosecutor—because he would not release information that Alan had requested concerning the operations of his office. The local newspaper identified Alan as a researcher hired by the campaign, and when the reporter called our office for comment, I answered the phone. He asked what we expected the records to show. I said, "Without seeing them, I have no idea what they'll show." Even that was more than I wanted to say.

The fact that we're doing research should never be the story; the findings are what matter. But the road has ears and you never know who's listening. Maybe a newspaper reporter, maybe another researcher, or maybe just a busybody. Alan and I have learned not to talk business while conducting business. That lesson presented itself one day in a hall-way outside of a county records room as we sat on a bench sorting through some property documents and discussing their importance.

"I know where that is," a voice suddenly said as I read off a street address to Alan. We looked up to see a woman staring at us. Not knowing who this person was and immediately feeling reckless for be-ing overheard in such a public place, we both nodded as Alan quickly said, "We've got it, thanks." Then we were gone.

There's no annual Opposition Researchers Convention that we know of, and even if there were, I feel confidant that no one would show. Just a banner, a table scattered with blank nametags and some empty chairs.

Party crossover among political researchers is limited, partly be-cause connections are with your own party, but mostly because it's a matter of commitment, loyalty and trust. We have worked for Repub-lican candidates only twice, both times in races where no Democrats were involved. It was oddly discomfiting, yet interesting to catch a glimpse of the inside of the opposing machine, which is no doubt an-other reason campaigns stick with researchers who share their ideol-ogy. It's like driving into a strange town, stopping for a moment to get your bearings so you can figure out exactly where you need to go next.

Single-party races are a breed of their own. It's tougher to develop contrasts between candidates when both have records of wreaking havoc on the environment or baselessly shouting down tax increases or condemning same-sex marriage. Which candidate owns more guns? Which one is more rabid about closing the gates on immigrants? Which one would outlaw abortion in every single instance? The hot-button issues that either party likes to bring to life during a campaign can become even hotter when they decide to go after one another.

Sometimes, the lines between good, bad and simply weird become hopelessly interwoven. The adage that "all politicians are the same" is far from true. No two are ever really alike. That fact was confirmed for me as I stood late one night on a ballroom dance floor as a candidate whom we were researching sashayed partnerless in fluid motions in front of me. I watched with a combination of awe, disbelief and wonderment.

Alan was off on a different project, and I'd met up with the candidate at a local restaurant to go through the usual list of questions we always ask at the beginning of a self-research project. After dinner, several cocktails and a lengthy conversation, I was asked to follow the candidate home to collect some documents I needed for my report. And, of course, I complied when I was invited to see the dance floor the candidate had built in the house. A mirrored orb hung from the ceiling and music played as the dancing demonstration commenced. I can only imagine that my expression at that moment was that of a dog with a slightly cocked head, staring in confusion at something it didn't quite understand or comprehend.

So I just watched, trying to smile pleasantly and nod as the dancing candidate swooshed past me and back again. Any normal person would have been asking himself the same questions: How in the hell did I get here? When can I leave? Is this person going to ask me to dance as well? Please, God, no.

While dancing candidates may be the exception, the element of strangeness they lend to our work can be curiously refreshing amid weeks of plowing through pages of often-dry information. And if someone's willing to two-step across a dance floor in front of you in the middle of the night, that person is most likely going to be pretty open about themselves, which makes our job a little easier.

Such was not the case with our Florida congressional candidate who had just finished chewing me out over the phone during a conversation that was supposed to be routine. "I'll get back to you on the research," he told me as he hung up. He never did.

Sure enough, just as I tried to explain to him, his opponent in the race discovered the information he'd believed could somehow be kept hidden if he didn't hire us to do the research. According to the local newspaper, the candidate had been accused by his opponent of cheating several people out of tens of thousands of dollars several years back. One of those he reportedly cheated came forward to share his story.

The candidate told the paper that he was "astonished" that his opponent would stoop to such dirty politics. But no one else was, including us.

A few days after he lost the race, Alan and I got a note from the now-former campaign manager, who said it was finally clear why the candidate shunned the research, because then he would have had to test it in a poll, and word would have gotten out. He'd told the candidate that he would be attacked, but he refused to believe it. He got pissed off, the manager said, arguing that since they hadn't attacked him when he was the mayor, they wouldn't go after him when he ran for Congress.

If only those bowling balls would all land in the same place. . . .

13
Alan

The security line at the New Orleans city hall is maddeningly slow. New Orleans officially refers to itself, without irony, as the City that Care Forgot. The city claims both the highest percentage of native-born residents and the highest murder rate in the United States, which says something about familiarity; if you have the misfortune to get shot there, you have a greater chance of knowing your assailant than elsewhere. It also helps explain why the locals are prone to confusing weapons searches with opportunities to get caught up with each other.

Only a visitor from the oddly caring universe beyond Lake Pontchartrain would object to such interruptions of daily life as being stranded in traffic during carnival season by the umpteenth miles-long parade snaking its way through the city, blocking every possible transportation route, during which an old woman riding in a grocery cart, dressed entirely in feather boas and pushed by a man wearing only a chef's apron, proceeds to slosh beer on the hood of our car and shout, with surprising gusto, "Go to hell, assholes! Happy Mardi Gras!"

The response of the cop on the corner? "Happy Mardi Gras, Colleen!"

Passing through the slo-mo security line at city hall requires the presentation of photo ID and, judging from what we observe up ahead, chatting with the guards about Reggie Jackson and someone's auntie's recipe for crawfish étouffée, utterly mindless of the fact that there are twelve people waiting behind you in line. No one else seems bothered in the slightest by this, but by the time my turn to pass through the security screen comes, I've become nostalgic for care. In part, this is because Michael insisted that we stay out the night before until 3:00 AM drinking whiskey and dropping cash like drug dealers in what turned out to be a pretty awesome strip club. And I say that as someone who normally hates that kind of place. I ended up leaving before Michael, and the walk home, down Bourbon Street, had been a surreal slice of avant-garde cinema verité starring heat-seeking prostitutes, rent boys and drag queens—the only other pedestrians out at that time on a weeknight, who responded to my passage by launching themselves toward me, one after the other, while issuing a succession of profane offers and ultimatums. I'd never seen so many gold teeth up close.

This coterie of furies hounded me all the way back to the Bourbon Orleans Hotel, where the last of them finally fell away, muttering in loud dismay. A few short hours later, Michael and I received our wake-up calls in the form of light knocks on our respective doors, followed by the familiar command, "Housekeeping!" Multiple cups of strong coffee served only to send waves of agitation through the ransacked temples of our bodies, and did nothing to prepare us for this security line. My head is pounding, I feel a little wobbly and I've begun to sweat profusely. Michael can barely speak.

When I finally arrive at the stool on which the uniformed policeman is receiving company, she looks at my Mississippi driver's license and very noticeably frowns. I'm not talking about a look of minor disapproval; I'm talking about an expression that requires exertion. I know where this is going, and I'm not up for it. My discomfort with being awake and forced to work has been waiting for just such a moment to find its voice.

The cop, still nursing her theatrical frown, hands my license back to me, positions her other hand on her hip—the universal signal for "I don't *think* so," and levels on me a gaze that aptly conveys her complete dissatisfaction with the geography of my birth. Not only am I from beyond the boundaries of the known world (i.e., past Lake Pontchartrain), I'm from Mississippi, where the state flag incorporates the Confederate symbol.

Which is true. I viewed the civil rights era from the vantage point of a white child in Mississippi, which is to say I assumed that families the world over passed the smoldering ruins of fire-bombed churches in their station wagons on the way to Mammaw's house. It was only later, as a teenager, that I realized something had actually been terribly, uniquely wrong. Over time, despite my lack of culpability, I became accustomed to occasionally serving as a convenient scapegoat for civil rights–era crimes, typically by people in the North. (Although I once received a reprimand from a *German*, to whom I responded that if my homeland had been responsible for the Holocaust I would most assuredly keep my opinions about other people's human rights violations to myself.) I've come to terms with this. However, on this particular morning, I'm not feeling very agreeable when the cop expresses her unspoken yet obvious displeasure with the state that authorized me to drive.

"What?" I demand to know. Basically asking for it.

"Mississippi—that's a state I don't like. Done some bad things to black folks," she says. "Mm hmm. Sure did."

I'm thinking, "OK, the judges will accept that. Some very bad things were done to black people in Mississippi way back when. But now I'm supposed to hear about it from someone in Louisiana?"

"Like it wasn't bad in Louisiana!" I shoot back.

She stares at me for a long moment, thinking. Then, to my surprise, she grins, and in the beguiling dialect of the Lower Ninth Ward, or perhaps Treme, exclaims, "I heard *dat!* It was *worser* here," and gives me a high five. Afterward I feel as if I have passed through more than the security portal; I have now successfully entered one of the few places where New Orleans pretends to care—its *fraternité*. And with that, I am free to proceed into the city's disorganized, mildewed city hall. Little do I know that this right of passage will be the high point of my day.

"Where's the clerk's office?" Michael blurts out, preemptively, as I await him, just inside the perimeter. The guard points toward the elevator and summons the next visitor in line. She is satisfied, apparently, and barely gives Michael's driver's license a glance.

What follows is, for us, painful, made more so by the caustic mix of caffeine and slowly degrading alcohol coursing through our irregularly pulsing veins. Despite my momentary triumph in the security line, it is only with great difficulty that I can concentrate on the blurry records. At one point I leave the room and return to find Michael sound asleep with his head resting on a docket book, his briefcase open beside him, revealing a telltale tabletop sign decorated with daisies drawn in different colors of Sharpies, with the name "Amber" scrawled across in childish script—a gift from one of the dancers the night before.

Despite all of this, we soon begin finding great stuff, tying our candidate's campaign contributors to the awarding of government contracts—a surprisingly common enterprise among elected officials, as you may have noticed. Our somnambulant success stems from a healthy matrix, I like to think. It's not so much that we could actually do it in our sleep as that even when we're weary—for whatever reason—we know how to get on the ride. We are not easily diverted, even by our own efforts to find diversion. An evening spent in consort with strippers, followed by a morning spent enduring low-grade agitation in the bowels of a musty government building, is oddly conducive to our kind of work. In the best cases, our off-road forays actually serve to rejuvenate us, preventing us from becoming oppo automatons—the functional equivalent of computerized search engines. We are, ultimately, two naturally subjective guys with an unwaveringly objective agenda.

The problem with our New Orleans effort is that everything about it—the actual work and our quest for collateral entertainment—is so relentlessly productive. It's hard to keep it up around the clock. Such are the hazards of attempting to balance the execution of gravely important, occasionally mind-numbing tasks with local stimulation. Sometimes we go too far. But the work should be fun. Life is short.

Our two weeks in New Orleans follows a particularly enervating stint in Baton Rouge, which had left us yearning for stimulation. Most state capitals are uniformly bland government towns, but you'd expect Baton Rouge to be an exception, Louisiana being a culturally rich state where people aren't at all surprised when their governor serves time. And yet, in Baton Rouge we endured a week of institutional doldrums, eating the same Chinese buffet every day, spending countless hours combing through legislative journals, breathing fumes from the petrochemical refineries that line the riverfront. At one point Michael began loudly pounding on a broken copy machine at the state library, which caused something of a stir. It's pretty obvious when we're getting worn down by a summer of nonstop, highly detailed trouble. New Orleans is close to home, but we're here for two weeks, and what's next up I can't even remember now.

During the height of the campaign season we're gone more than we're home, returning every few weeks for a few days to pay bills, touch base with friends and family, finalize our latest oppo report, search the web for hotels and restaurants and addresses and whatever at our next destination—all while fielding calls from campaign staffers and consultants eager to know when we'll finish our work or wanting follow-up research, or setting up conference calls with pollsters who need assurance that their questions are supported by our documentation. The pace doesn't slow from May to October. Our lives become a blur of airport terminals, highway signs, building directories and document files. At one point I ended up in Arizona, and I no longer even recall why. All I remember is burning my fingers on the rental car's door handle because it was so hot, and staying in a nice hotel at the base of a mesa.

Touring the country like this can make us feel like *Natural Born Researchers* on an interstate rampage. We may research twenty candidates in a single summer, and the travel, the research and dealing with the campaigns can be intense. It's all so negative, and even we have our limits. At such times the need for entertainment becomes more pronounced, particularly after spending hours on an interstate highway in a cheap rental car that weaves unpredictably. We often take the long way back to our hotel in hopes of happening on some odd roadside attraction, such as our encounter with Chatty Belle, the World's Largest Talking Cow, a fiberglass bovine that stood proudly beside her mute, vandalized calf on a Wisconsin highway shoulder, not far from an empty tractor-trailer that once held the largest replica piece of cheese in history—seventeen tons of it—in honor of the real hunk of cheese that was featured at the 1964 World's Fair.

A lot of what passes for opposition research today is done exclusively on the web by people with no real knowledge of the local context, but we, for many reasons, find it useful to get to know a place, up close and personal. It's not only because the web is notoriously unreliable, and that some records aren't available online. It's also because you get a better sense of the context. Any reporter will tell you that you get a better story when you go to the scene of the action, rather than conduct interviews over the phone. Though she never came out and said it, Chatty Belle was clearly repping for the dairy lobby, which hinted that our subject candidate's history of voting for dairy price supports might not cause much consternation there.

Invariably there's a lot of free time, after the government offices close for the day and on weekends, and at such times we may find ourselves piloting a rented boat on a shimmering Minnesota lake or hanging on every sonorous word uttered by a beautiful Creole woman leading a tour of a Mississippi River plantation house (one of the rare occasions when we opted to take the guided tour). It's definitely more fun when the nature of the research calls for us to travel together, though on solo trips there's a better chance of meeting and getting to know someone new.

The trips offer a view of the United States we wouldn't otherwise be likely to see. Our vantage point is much like it was of the Statue of Liberty that day in Jersey City—from behind. We see homeless people in Des Moines, staggering down the street with their shoulders hunched and heads down, while the candidate we're researching is off in Washington, voting to subsidize the multinational corporations that fund his campaigns. In Cedar Rapids we pass a group of cocky young guys working on a car in the parking lot of the Tastee Freez, as if transplanted from a Bruce Springsteen song, and notice that the whole town smells like cereal, owing to the Ralston and Quaker Oats mills. In Dallas we visit the Texas Book Depository and gaze out the window from which Lee Harvey Oswald shot JFK; in DC we stop at the Dupont Hilton on Embassy Row and see the spot where Reagan was shot. In Minneapolis we visit what used to be the great falls of the Mississippi, which have eroded away, and I imagine the eagle aeries that once were clustered around the falls, which were held sacred by the Dakotas but are now supplanted by parks and the ruins of factories; meanwhile, a few blocks away, stands a ridiculous statue of Mary Tyler Moore throwing her hat into the air—an example of local culture defining itself by imagery invented by TV.

Beyond finding something useful for the campaigns, we're inspired by seeing how the behavior of local politicians illustrates what's going on in America—how politics influences and is influenced by the people we meet or observe along the way. We compile our cultural audits from a variety of sources, and have gotten pretty good at finding entertainment along the way, though sometimes both endeavors are challenging—for reasons vastly different than in New Orleans. Sadly, many places, including most of the midwestern corn belt, are studies in bad architecture and soul-sapping ennui. In such cases we sometimes resort to inventing games, such as searching for quirky businesses and signs. In particular, for some reason, we've focused on beauty parlor names: Hair Explosion, Glitz International by Mavis, Hair by the Sea, Shabazz Hair Care Oasis of Red Lick. One of the salons was close to home—Tina's Magnificent Beauty Closet, so we were aware when it later burned, and was rebuilt as, simply, Tina's Beauty Closet, the magnificence apparently having gone up in flames.

It's now possible to motor from Florida to Maine on a single multi-lane highway without seeing much of anything, passing through an interstate sensory deprivation zone that reveals the actual skyline of only one city, New York. While it's true that politics is, as they say, local, it's like so much about modern culture in that it's becoming increasingly franchised. You see many of the same basic political ads from coast to coast, produced by big agencies and blithely customized for specific races, just as you find heretically bland "Tuscan" dishes on the menus of a succession of chain Italian restaurants across four time zones. Michael and I try to seek out the local specialties, which sometimes poses a challenge. In Green Bay, when Michael asked a waitress what the local specialty was, she answered, "Fried cheese." When he protested that a person can get fried cheese anywhere, she replied, "Not made with fresh Wisconsin cheese!" Thank God for Walleye Wednesdays.

Occasionally, as in Miami's South Beach, our tandem searches for political ammunition and diversion coalesce. In Miami the tendency to groom one's image—a staple of politics—reaches what is perhaps its highest expression in the United States, with the possible exception of LA. Everyone we encountered was young, good-looking, rich and bad, except us. We were reduced to cruising Ocean Boulevard in our rented Kia, a horrid little plum-colored car in which we later suffered the indignity of a blowout on Tampa's Sunshine Skyway Bridge, after which we limped into chic Ybor City on the doughnut wheel. Not that it's necessarily a bad thing to view things from the outside. We were at once attracted to, yet hypervigilant of, South Florida's love of bone structure and bling, aware that a culture built on money and good looks carries its own unique political temptations.

The first candidate we researched in South Florida was classically handsome, with gym muscles bulging beneath his suit—the kind of guy everyone notices when he walks into the room. We were pleased to find that he had also been cited fifteen times for blowing through tollbooths without paying, and for running stop signs and speeding in, by turns, his Cadillac and his Jaguar. Another candidate voted five times to approve $170 million worth of contracts for a company with which she was associated. Crime being a big deal in South Florida, we were intrigued to discover a judge who would not sign a search warrant in the middle of the night when detectives had a chance to recover fifteen stolen guns, including an assault rifle, from a West Palm Beach apartment. The judge was so angry to have been awakened at 3:30 AM that he refused to sign the warrant. By the time the deputies got their warrant, six hours later, the guns were gone. Six weeks later, one of the guns the police had been prevented from confiscating was used to kill a twenty-two-year-old man. I think of this story when I hear people complain that they're tired of negative politics.

Considering the wide variation in locations, Michael and I occasionally disagree over who will go where on individual research projects. We travel together when the deadline and the sheer volume of work require it, but we often separate to undertake different campaigns simultaneously. When that happens, I usually manage to go to the more interesting places, in part because I know how Michael's mind works. I may point out that it makes sense to do the Seattle research and the San Francisco research over the course of one trip, and by the way I know someone I can stay with in the Bay Area, which will save us hundreds of dollars in hotel expenses. Over time, Michael has become more mindful of the disparities, realizing that while he's watching Pay-Per-View TV in his interstate hotel room I'm floating in someone's pool in Marin County. So he occasionally balks. He once insisted that we flip a coin. I won the toss, which meant I got to travel to New York City for two weeks while he was awarded a round trip ticket to Pikeville, Kentucky.

"I just saw something about Pikeville on the History Channel a few nights ago," Michael mused, trying to look impressed at his good fortune.

"Fascinating," I said, as I began Googling Manhattan hotels.

Pikeville, he pointed out, was where the Hatfields and the McCoys engaged in their legendary feud, which started with a dispute over a hog. He said he could see by the look on my face that I was awed by his arcane knowledge of regional history, adding, "Sometimes I even surprise myself. I think it'll be interesting."

As it turned out, he could not sustain his air of triumph for long. It proved fun, for a minute, to discover Pikeville's quiet horrors, one gap-toothed records clerk at a time. During our regular status updates, I gloated about researching my candidate in the same courthouse that appears in scenes of *Law and Order* and dancing into the wee hours with a stranger in a SoHo bar. I could tell he'd reached his breaking point when, as I was trying to explain how I'd happened on Jerry Seinfeld the night before, waiting in line for the premier of a show, and how we'd exchanged the wussup nod, he interrupted to say, quite petulantly, "Oh, really. Have you had any time to do any actual work? Because I can assure you there are no celebrities in Pikeville, Kentucky."

Softening, I reminded him that the process of discovery matters equally in the world's busiest and most culturally diverse city as in some hillbilly town founded long ago when a random pioneer's wagon broke down. At this point he was forced to concede that he had also come up with nothing that mattered for the campaign. "It's because I'm in a shitty place," he said.

It made matters worse that I had tapped into some great information in New York. Michael prides himself on finding the best information—we often compete in that regard, and it's true that he tends to be discerning and methodical, while I discover things in a more scattershot manner—but in Pikeville, he'd come up with nothing that mattered for the campaign. I'd found where one of our opponents, whose campaign platform was that he would operate government "like a business," had had five federal tax liens filed against his own commercial enterprise, which had also been sued twice for unpaid debts. Meanwhile, across the river in New Jersey, I'd found where a state police investigator who was running for office had been restrained during an altercation with a group of local cops, during which he had used racial slurs, and another candidate who'd been fined $13,000 for violating state campaign finance laws while treasurer of his party's county organization.

After I relayed these details, there was silence on the other end of the line. Finally, Michael sighed and said, "I've been eating greasy tacos from a gas station, and all there is to do at night is watch *Andy Griffith* reruns. And I swear there's bloodstains on the wall of my motel room. The worst part is that there's just nothing."

Now and then we become so immersed in far-flung research projects that we wake up wondering where we are. Sometimes we momentarily forget where we're going while airborne. We are occasionally beset by flight delays, including, in one case, when we were forced to stay overnight in a dreaded airport hotel in Atlanta, without our bags, and to fly out the next day for a meeting with a congressman dressed in wrinkled, dirty clothes. When we got to Minneapolis our rental car reservation had been canceled, forcing us to scrounge for another. When we arrived at our hotel they refused to refund the money we had prepaid, though they'd given our room away. When we finally found other accommodations, the valet wrecked our car. Such stresses are part of the process, but the parade of odd characters and memorable scenes provides a welcome antidote to—as well as entertaining context for—the information we gather.

Typically, the campaigns we work for don't fully understand why, as we're researching their opponents, we're also chronicling the trail of outlaw Jesse James. Our position is that whether you're following an actual historic trail, touring a stylized mockup or blazing your own path, it's all about outlaws and lawmen, about who's right and who's wrong. The evidence is wherever you find it—however you find it.

As much as it's influenced by national trends, political behavior can be very site specific, so, in a way, all of this matters. One of the more unusual places we've done oppo is Utah, which looks homogenous on the surface but becomes far more complicated once you're inside. Utah is much like you might picture it: high, dry and populated primarily by clean-cut, square-jawed Mormons whose ancestors wanted to get away from everyone else. Those ancestors resorted to violence when disputes arose with Native American tribes and the U.S. government itself and, in one bloody episode, slaughtered 120 settlers from Arkansas and Missouri, en route to California, whom they considered some kind of threat.

Because Mormonism emphasizes strict adherence to doctrine, and that doctrine strives to harness and limit individual power, you'd be safe assuming that Utah's demographic is pretty clearly defined. The state is more than 90 percent white and largely conservative. Yet there's a very visible counterculture of tattooed mountain bikers, dreadlocked backpackers and homeless vagabonds wandering Salt Lake City in clothes stained the color of desert canyons, wood smoke and industrial grime. Interspersed among the legions of men in starched white shirts who stroll West Temple Street are a remarkable number of guys wearing no shirts at all. Cultural escape takes many forms in Utah: Sometimes it's shirts; sometimes it's skins.

The alternative types stand out in Utah precisely because the mainstream culture, while deviating in significant ways from the American norm, is very staid. When I was there researching a congressional candidate I saw an alt-guy with his alt-girl dressed in dirty, torn, gray-and-olive-drab clothes, scuffed hiking boots and head rags that looked as if they'd been ripped from the drapes of an abandoned building. Their hair was wild and dirty. The scent of campfires and long-term B.O. lingered in their wake as they passed a café where four Mitt Romney clones were dining al fresco. At that moment, Utah felt like no place I'd ever been. It's as if the survivors of some postapocalyptic world had wandered on to the set of the old *Osmond Family Show*.

When I mentioned the odd contrast of Donny-and-Marie-meet-Mad-Max to my friend Edy, who lives in nearby Park City, she said, "That would be a street fight worth watching." Her money would be on the Mormons, she said, because they could disable the road warriors with laserlike smiles bright enough to glint off the windows of downtown buildings.

Surprisingly, though, there didn't seem to be much conflict. For one thing, all those young Mormons you see roaming the neighborhoods of other cities, proselytizing in their telltale shirts and ties, are actually outliers of a deeply entrenched bike-centric civilization that, in Utah, encompasses both mainstream and alternative lifestyles. In Salt Lake you see bicycles everywhere, piloted by people of all ages and backgrounds—men in suits, women in shorts and sandals, road-weary travelers laden with cross-country baggage, mountain trekkers outfitted with technical gear, delivery guys, elderly eccentrics, kids. Despite the familiar American car culture that periodically smothers Salt Lake in a haze of pollution and contributes to sprawl throughout the valley, there's a strong athletic vibe that also carries a whiff of anarchy. This is a society, after all, where polygamy was once considered a family value.

Famous people with Utah connections are an odd assortment: Butch Cassidy, Donny and Marie, serial killer Ted Bundy, Robert Redford, Mitt Romney and Karl Rove. There's also that guy who kidnapped Elizabeth Smart and kept her in a pen in his backyard. If you can find the median in that demographic, have at it. What this all means to a political researcher is that whatever you find on a candidate will have to fit into a very narrow box. Social issues aren't likely to bring a serious candidate down because the vast majority of the population believes pretty much the same thing. Anyone who looks the least bit crazy, meanwhile, isn't going to have a chance. The question is what, exactly, the majority of the voters believe, in the aggregate.

For a politician, playing to an audience that is both mainstream and slightly renegade carries inherent yet ill-defined risks, but on the ground in Utah, it was clear that the worst thing we could discover about a candidate was that he did not play by the rules. Mormonism places particular emphasis on abiding by a host of rules, many of which are unique to the religion. The inevitable backlash is about flagrantly breaking them. Not surprisingly, the candidate I was in town to research hadn't been obvious about his violations. He had sidled up to the Tea Party crowd, the antiabortionists and the like, but aside from breaking some of the rules of conventional American politics, those associations didn't look particularly controversial. His public statements generally reflected predictable rightwing opinions, with a few twists. He'd opposed a bill to ban gifts from lobbyists, while accepting such gifts himself, which said something about him but did not indicate inconsistency—another trait that puts off many Mormon voters. There were a few other minor problems, such as that he had missed more than two hundred votes while a state legislator. But his most egregious offense was something more personal, and that was not easily discovered: a tax lien filed against him for failing to pay state income tax—an indication that he had, in fact, violated the rules.

The lien wasn't really out there for public consumption. While going through the index of lawsuits the candidate was involved in I found one reference without a clear description, though the index code (as a helpful staffer in the state law library explained) indicated it was a tax lien. Utah has strict privacy laws that make it one of the more difficult places where Michael and I have ever done research. Finding and acquiring copies of even routine documents can be a clerical Rubik's Cube of confusing guidelines, and it's not uncommon to get conflicting reports from staffers in the same office about what is public record. In the case of the tax lien, the woman at the window of the court clerk's office flatly refused to let me see it.

"Is it not a public record?" I asked, cutting to the chase.

It was, she said, but it contained private information that could not be disclosed. Here then, was one of those "special" records: a public-private one, which was technically available but could not actually be seen. In the end, after much pleading and, at one point, my suggestion that perhaps someone higher up might be able to settle the issue, the woman at the window at least told me that the case did, in fact, involve a lien for failure to pay state income tax, albeit for property in another state. The exact address she wouldn't give me. It wasn't entirely satisfying, but it was enough. So much for the fiscal responsibility platform, dude.

As with any club, the membership rules of the Utah voting district were at times inscrutable, and subject to change. There was no huge controversy in the candidate's background, and he couldn't exactly be portrayed as a danger to the fold, but there were clues that could be discerned up close, on the ground. Bits and pieces that emerged in the race, including that tax lien, were enough to convince the voters that he was less attractive than the incumbent, whose personal political doctrines were known. In the end, the opponent lost.

Utah was a perfect example of why it's risky to research candidates from the quiet sanctuary of your office. People often ask Michael and me how the expansion of the Internet has changed the way we do our work, and the answer is that in some ways it has simplified things, as it has for everyone. Many of the records we once had to dig up in libraries and newspaper or courthouse archives are now available online. But it has also complicated things by moving the debate further from that documentation, and it has meanwhile given people—including some who work for political campaigns—a false sense of understanding of the issues at hand. Campaigns may operate under the assumption that they can come up with a list of search words, assign a volunteer to Google the necessary documentation and build their case around that. But there, in Salt Lake City, was the contraindication. Even on the ground I was only able to get bits and pieces, and the most telling among them never came up during any of our Internet searches.

The Internet seems to be supplanting every other conduit and repository of information, but everything is not there yet and I'm not sure it ever will be. The life of a place and the life of a candidate do not unfold electronically.

14

Michael

My first thought on this cold and rainy Monday morning is that there's no possible way I can crawl out of this bed. And if I do, I'll just fall on the floor and die anyway. Oh sure, they'll find me, but not until they break down the hotel door days from now.

Anyone who's ever worked on the road has thought about the possibility of this happening. I had felt it coming the day before on my flight to the Northwest but convinced myself for the moment that it would pass. All these years traveling and never once had I been really sick. The plastic thermometer I bought when I landed now read 102. My meeting with the candidate and his campaign people was at 8:00 AM. What was I supposed to do?

"I'm sorry. I know you flew me two thousand miles and are paying me all this money to conduct this research, but I'm not really feeling well, so I think I'll just stay here in this great hotel you're paying for and sleep."

No, I have to go. There are deadlines to meet. It's all about deadlines. The temperature outside is hovering in the thirties and I'm on fire as I take my seat a noninfectious distance away from the candidate and his campaign manager at a breakfast meeting, where we begin going over their suggestions and ideas. Everything is blurry. Every fiber of my body feels like a rubber band stretched to its popping point.

If self-combustion can, indeed, occur, then I am just minutes away from becoming a smoldering ash pile on the floor beneath my plate of scrambled eggs.

"Are you OK?" the manager asks in a somewhat sympathetic-sounding tone while looking puzzled over my apparent lack of coherency in answering their questions.

"Yeah, I'm fine. Just a little tired I guess from the trip yesterday," I reply.

But who am I kidding? If I look as bad as I feel, I'm not kidding anyone. The first day is the worst. Even without the flu, there's the added stress of getting your bearings in a new town and locating all the places you'll need to go to collect information. Mondays are always tough, and though I'm certain I'll perish at any time, I manage to make it through this one and stumble back to my hotel—to a bottle of aspirin and room service. All I want is a bowl of hot soup, and the only kind they serve is split pea. So that's what I get, as I will every night for the next week.

The following morning I awake shivering. I'm a degree hotter and I begin to worry about something someone once told me about high body temperatures: that a person's brain can actually begin to cook and sizzle and finally just melt. I had bought a fuzzy green stocking cap stamped with some unfamiliar logo the day before at a drugstore. The thought of my brain melting into something already so unattractive is scary and depressing. But I'm cold, so I put it on, along with a pair of jeans over a pair of sweat pants I had packed with the intent to go for a run. A t-shirt covered by a dress shirt covered by a hooded sweatshirt covered by a sport coat blanket my upper body. I rarely drink coffee, but today I gulp as much as I can muster and head out again, hoping the caffeine will keep me standing.

"May I help you?" asks a courthouse clerk on my first stop of the day. I can't figure out why she's staring at my feet until I look down to notice that my sweatpants are about three inches longer than the bottom of my jeans. She must think I'm wearing pajamas. I don't care.

"Yes, ma'am, I'm looking for some tax information." She moves her eyes between my green hat and my ankles and speaks to me in a tone that is alternately filled with pity and wariness.

It's like that everywhere I go. Security guards ask me why I'm here; government employees don't know whether to help me or ask me to leave. As I walk past the reflective window of an office building I get my first full look at myself. If I didn't feel so wretched, I would laugh. My appearance lies somewhere between homeless and mentally challenged. A mentally challenged homeless man who wants to see all the tax records on a political candidate. In a way it's helpful because no one takes me very seriously. For the first time I can remember, no one asks me who I'm with or for whom I work. Mentally challenged homeless guys are never with anybody. As I trudge the streets from building to building, I expect someone to hand me some spare change at any moment.

On my fourth flu night, I call down for room service. By now they know me.

"Good evening! Split pea tonight?"

"Is that really all you have?" I ask hopefully.

"It's our specialty," he replies in a cheery tone.

"Isn't there maybe a can of chicken noodle stuck on the back of a shelf somewhere?" I plead.

"We have our Chicken Oscar that's very good. But it's not a soup."

"Just bring me the split pea."

Anyone who's ever eaten split pea soup knows that a week's worth is a gastronomical nightmare. Split peas are actually dried, peeled and split seeds. And though they're a great source of protein, they also contain certain sugars that our digestive enzymes are incapable of breaking apart for absorption. Once in the lower intestine, the sugars are metabolized and form carbon dioxide, hydrogen and, yes, methane gas.

This combination of flu and extreme intestinal discomfort proves particularly troublesome when part of my research uncovers the fact that the opposing candidate owns a restaurant that's been cited more than a hundred times for health code violations. The suggestion is made that I visit this restaurant for lunch. All that's going through my mind is the thought of those health inspectors who found mold in the ice machines, cockroach infestations, employees washing their hands without soap, and food preparation sinks directly connected to the raw sewage system. I'm more than queasy. A person's dedication to his job can go only so far and I believe I've done my duty. There's nothing in the job description that states I have to subject myself to this (or keep subjecting the public to me). But then I wonder if they might serve a nice broth.

Sick or not, there are no excuses in political campaigns. Time is too short and the stakes are too high. When you've got two weeks left to finish a project, as I do on this one, no one cares how you feel. The job comes first and you get it done. It's all about deadlines. You live by deadlines and you can most certainly die by deadlines.

The word "deadline" actually has a deadly origin dating back to the Civil War. In the official records of the Union and Confederate armies is an obscure inspection report from Confederate captain Walter Bowie dated May 10, 1864. The report describes conditions at the infamous prisoner-of-war camp for Union soldiers at Andersonville, Georgia. In it, Bowie wrote, "On the inside of the stockade and twenty feet from it there is a dead-line established, over which no prisoner is allowed to go, day or night, under penalty of being shot."

The word, of course, has evolved into simply meaning a time limit to complete some activity. And though crossing a deadline today generally won't result in being shot, it can sometimes feel like it. Alan and I have worked under more deadlines than we can count since our days as reporters.

The most brutal editor for whom I ever worked was a city editor who was terrified of our managing editor. Her way of trying to please him was to feed him as many news stories in a day as possible, much like throwing meat at a hungry tiger. She would take stories from other cities and attempt to "localize" them, inventing some idiotic angle that she believed would interest our readers. Two hours before deadline she would lay two more story assignments on my desk. An hour before deadline there would be another. Thirty minutes before deadline one more might find its way over.

"See if you can make a few calls on this," she would say. It was her favorite line and I came to despise it. I learned then that deadlines can do two things to people: They can paralyze us into total inaction or they can bring out our best efforts. It's all in the way we handle them.

Deadlines bring about rushes of energy from the adrenaline they unleash. The exact scientific actions on the body are complicated, involving receptors and glands and organs and secretions. The heart beats faster; breathing is more rapid; energy levels are higher. Adrenaline is great. Hell, they even give it to you if you're in cardiac arrest.

Alan always tells people, "We live for deadlines." He's right. The political seasons in which we work are, for the most part, about six months of continuous deadlines. The actual core research we conduct for each campaign takes between three and five weeks. We have always touted our ability to meet deadlines and provide quick turnarounds. In eighteen years we've never crossed a deadline yet—never been shot or even fired upon. To expand on the famous motto of the U.S. Postal Service: Neither snow nor rain nor heat nor flu stay these couriers from the swift completion of their appointed rounds.

Deadlines are finite, but their importance is relative. Everyone has them and most everyone believes theirs are tougher or more important than the next guy's. I know I do. It is true, however, that missing any deadline carries a cost. A few years ago in California, a large corporation was told by a judge that it wasn't entitled to $1 million in attorney's fees for a case it won because its attorneys were literally sixty seconds late in filing the legal paperwork required to collect those fees. More specifically, the law firm's courier was late because the attorney in charge of filing the paperwork waited until forty-six minutes before the deadline to give it to the courier who then got stuck in traffic and had to wait at a rail crossing for a long train to pass. When he arrived at the courthouse it was closed. The judge in the case wrote that, though regrettable, "The entirely foreseeable obstacle of traffic in Southern California in the late afternoon . . . cannot justify an enlargement in time." In other words: You missed the deadline; it's your loss.

It is ironic in a way that the candidates Alan and I assist by adhering to our and their strict deadlines end up employed by one of the worst deadline-missing organizations in the world: the federal government.

"If you don't set a deadline in this town, nothing happens," President Obama said in 2009, right before Congress missed a deadline to pass his health care reform. An administration sets deadlines and Congress ignores them, largely without consequence. Obama warned Congress in 2009 to pass health care reform by that August. It didn't happen until March 2010. The deadline for closing the prison at Guantánamo Bay was the end of the president's first year in office. It didn't happen.

"Any talk of deadlines is an absolute waste of time," one Democratic senator said.

The federal government even managed to miss all thirty-four deadlines set by Congress for requiring energy-efficiency standards for consumer products, costing Americans tens of billions of dollars more for energy. But while our government may miss its own deadlines, it doesn't look kindly on us when we do it. Wait until after April 15 to mail your income tax return and see what happens. Even failing to complete the ten-year U.S. Census form on time carries the threat of a fine. Try having to explain how you got busted for a census violation on your next job application form.

Miss enough deadlines and you get replaced, unless of course you're the only one who can do your job. Just ask BP. A month after the Deepwater Horizon drilling rig exploded in the Gulf of Mexico, causing the largest man-made oil spill in U.S. history, Interior Secretary Ken Salazar blasted the giant petroleum producer, saying BP had blown "deadline after deadline" in its efforts to stop the leak. Yet, at the same time, the federal government acknowledged that it had to rely on the company's equipment and expertise to close the hole. It's like a drunken tow truck driver who causes a massive multicar pileup in the middle of town. Sure, says the police chief, we'd like to arrest him, but he's got the only tow truck in the city and he's the only one who knows how to drive it.

The challenge is to know when a deadline is getting in the way of what really matters, when it's going to prevent you from pursuing a late-breaking lead. Also tricky: believing you can meet multiple deadlines by possessing the ability to do more than one thing at the same time. No one possesses that ability. It's a myth. Studies consistently show that the human brain cannot fully focus on more than one thing at a time. We may be able to shift our focus faster than somebody else can shift theirs and believe we're doing two things at once, but that's about it. And even then it's tough to maintain effectiveness at each task. The next time you're at a sporting event or a party, try holding a conversation with the person next to you while listening to the conversation of the person on the other side at the same time. Then, just for fun, trying doing it drunk.

When we're working on four or five campaigns at once, shifting focus (and occasionally drinking) becomes the only way to adhere to deadlines. There is no prioritizing. You can't tell yourself that one campaign is more important than another and, therefore, can wait. You can't not return calls from an anxious campaign manager in need of a quick parcel of information just because you're in the middle of another job. Several times Alan and I have been hired because the researcher who was initially brought on board couldn't be reached after he'd turned over his initial report. In this business, even after the deadline is met, you have to remember that nothing is over until the polls close.

Adrenaline is great for helping you meet deadlines, especially when you feel like crap. The problem is that, much like split pea soup, you can't subsist on it forever. In the end, it's unsustainable. Fortunately for me, this hellish week has ended and I'm actually beginning to feel better. As I leave the hotel room, I toss my fuzzy green stocking cap in the trash. It had been a good cap but its usefulness has reached an end and I don't plan on ever wearing it again.

"God, what happened to you?" Alan says when I walk into the office on Monday morning. He already knows, of course, but it's his way of acknowledging that I'd had a tough trip.

By the end of the week, I send my research report to the campaign, which not only details the health code violations that put restaurant patrons at risk, but it also chronicles a candidate who, while portraying himself as an experienced businessman and community leader, has a history of concealing serious financial troubles. He has put others at financial risk for his own gain, including using money from a trust fund he oversaw to cover his mounting debts, and he has a host of problems paying his taxes.

Alan and I almost never toss compliments at one another. It's just not our nature. Over the years, we have simply come to understand that each of us knows the business, the deadlines and how to get it all done. We've never needed each other's approval. So a few days later, as he's leaving work, I'm somewhat taken aback when he turns and says, "You know, that was a really good report. You did a good job."

"Let's just hope our guy wins," I reply.

He does.

15

Alan

In the mideighties, the state of Mississippi, which later served as our
proving ground as opposition researchers, was in the throes of a particularly brutal, and surreal, gubernatorial election. At the center
stood a trio of transvestite prostitutes who claimed they'd had sex, on
numerous occasions, with the leading candidate, a Democrat who was
then the state attorney general. Notably, considering where we were, the
prostitutes were black and the AG was white.

I was a reporter in Jackson at the time, and the newspaper's statewide editor, a fiery former marine and Vietnam War veteran, su-
pervised the coverage of the story, which attracted a national media
circus that included Geraldo Rivera, the controversial correspondent
for the ABC News show *20/20*. During a particularly aggressive interview, Rivera, a proud pioneer of trash TV, drove one of the transvestites to tears by angrily demanding to know how it felt to have
"ruined a man's life." It was, in a way, a legitimate question, particularly considering the transvestites' penchant for changing their
stories, but his delivery was unnecessarily rough. On-camera, the
transvestites came across as physically striking, yet they were shy, and
clearly unprepared for what they were getting into when they agreed
to vogue with the Republican businessmen who hired them to go
public with their stories.

The viciousness of Rivera's attack and the prostitute's resulting distress prompted my editor, who was present for the interview, to intercede. He and Rivera exchanged a few heated words and the argument devolved into a shoving match—a precursor to Rivera's brawl a few years later with skinheads, that famously earned him a broken nose. So it was that a freelance opposition research campaign undertaken by a group of conservative businessmen resulted in a Vietnam War vet fighting with Geraldo Rivera in defense of a sobbing transvestite. And that was just the offstage action.

The newspaper's executive editor had initially balked at reporting the results of the businessmen's inflammatory research, which they had privately presented to him. The group was comprised of longtime Republicans in what was then a staunchly Democratic state, and they clearly had a political vendetta against the AG. More importantly, there were significant questions about the veracity of their claims. Rather than accept the businessmen's word for it, the newspaper's editors assigned two reporters to investigate the matter independently.

The reporters discovered that the businessmen had hired a private detective agency to interview the prostitutes along with policemen who claimed to have seen the AG speaking with trolling prostitutes as they made their rounds. The businessmen then paid the transvestites to go public, and afterward sequestered them in various hotels across the Louisiana line, presumably to control access and to ensure they could find them when they needed them.

At the beginning, the Republican gubernatorial candidate steered clear of endorsing the businessmen's claims, though they were designed to get him elected. That would soon change. As the scandal reached a fever pitch, even his wife got in on it, smugly proclaiming during one speaking engagement, in reference to the fact that the attorney general was, you know, *divorced*, "I'm running for first lady, and I'm unopposed."

Ultimately, the lurid details, the shockingly personal nature of the attack, questions about the businessmen's payments to the prostitutes and attempts to convince the attorney general's financial donors to abandon him, together with the lack of clearly documented evidence, did not sit well with either the public or the media.

A reporter asked one of the businessmen during a news conference, "Are you attempting to ruin the man? Are you trying to defeat him? Are you trying to get him to withdraw? What are you doing?" Eventually, television and radio stations refused to sell the group airtime for their campaign ads, enabling the beleaguered attorney general to control the dialogue about the scandal. The result was that the Republican candidate's campaign was eclipsed by a bizarre sideshow staged by his own supporters.

Those of us in the newsroom found the scandal both riveting and sublimely wrong. I wasn't one of the reporters assigned to investigate it, but everyone in the newsroom was consumed by what was going down. For Michael and me, looking back as researchers, the obvious question is whether we would undertake such research for a campaign today. Our conclusion is that we would, initially, if only because it concerned a high law enforcement official allegedly breaking the law. But would we spy on the attorney general with night vision goggles or pay the transvestites for their story? No way. We're not private eyes. We'd interview the transvestites in hopes of documenting the allegations, but to purchase their stories would undermine the credibility of our findings, assuming there were any. Paying someone to create what *appeared* to be documentation is altogether different from documenting facts. If the allegations were impossible to prove, we'd advise the campaign to leave it alone. It would be up to them to decide what to do after that. We'd be on our way to the next race.

The most effective opposition research isn't necessarily the most shocking, particularly since few of us are truly shocked by much anymore. What work best are activities that stand in stark contrast to a candidate's public actions or stated positions on the issues. When a congressman gets caught sleeping with a female staffer, it's a bit worse if he's been touting abstinence education. If he's popular and handles the controversy well, the candidate may yet survive the onslaught, but no one likes a hypocrite. Regardless of their political persuasions, people like consistency, and inconsistency can be documented.

In today's world, where everything, it seems, is being documented, evidence of the disparities between a candidate's words and deeds is easier to come by. Almost everyone's phone has a camera and voice recorder. Video surveillance cameras track our daily routines. Sometimes we even reveal ourselves. It's not uncommon for mothers to post photos of their kids on Facebook, along with their names and the times they pick them up at school, for all the pedophiles of the world to see. The concept of privacy has been turned upside down. If you're a public figure, good luck sliding in and out of the shadows unnoticed for long.

It's not as if people are more prone to committing indiscretions today, sexual or otherwise, or to do so while holding press conferences about the importance of family values, whatever those are. It's just easier to document their behavior, and to frame it within the context of their perceived ability to lead. For our purposes, facts provide the foundation. But a candidate's missteps not only must be proved, they must also be significant to the broader issue of a candidate's fitness to serve. The danger, of course, is that in an age of rampant documentation, the documents can themselves be abused. Paragraphs or snippets of video can be taken out of context or even doctored to create a false set of "facts" that may then be embraced, unquestioningly, by the media and the general public. In such an environment, it's almost as if the "reader comments" on news sites and blogs are being authored by the same two angry people, one a conservative, one not, neither of whom is anyone you'd want to get stuck talking with at a party. Aside from not knowing the difference between "your" and "you're," they have one trait in common: their disregard for actual documented facts.

This combination of partisan fervor and disregard for facts helps explain how you end up with CNN, once a straight-up news organization, legitimizing a Tea Partier's claim that he'd unearthed "evidence" linking a newly crowned pageant winner whose greatest affront was to be Muslim with a reputed terrorist by the same last name, under the headline: MISS USA: MUSLIM TRAILBLAZER OR HEZBOLLAH SPY? Or how Fox News could run a video of the president saying taxes were going to go up substantially, after editing the snippet out of context to make it sound as if he were acknowledging the ramifications of his own policies rather than attributing the tax increase to his predecessor's, as he actually did. Politicians also respond in kind. The Obama administration, after all, forced USDA official Shirley Sherrod out of her job after a conservative web predator cynically edited a video of a speech she'd given about the importance of racial understanding. By making it seem that she'd said the opposite of what she had actually said, she came off sounding like a racist. Only later did the administration recognize that it had acted on a falsehood, and by then it was too late. If you need further evidence, in September 2009 an estimated 60,000 to 75,000 people showed up on the Mall in the nation's capital to protest Obama's political agenda. Conservative blogs ran photos purportedly taken at the event that showed a crowd of two million—photos that were, in fact, taken at a different, much larger march. Whether conservatives are more adept than liberals at such manipulations of reality is open for debate, but the point is that technology makes fabrication easy. It's more crucial than ever to verify the underlying source of the purported facts.

A police detective who gets caught tampering with factual evidence will likely get his case thrown out of court, but in the realm of politics, that same practice may be rewarded. Consider the following tidbit from Yahoo! News concerning Obama's decision to cancel a trip to the Sikh Golden Temple in India, ostensibly because he (or his advisers) was concerned about the possibility that photo ops of him wearing a weird, un-Christian head covering at a foreign, un-Christian religious site would go viral. Perhaps the potential for outrage, which the article sought to exploit, had precedent in the revulsion many Americans feel about one of their leaders curtsying before the Queen, but the Golden Temple is threatening only if you are wholly unfamiliar with Sikh culture.

Yahoo! began the Obama Sikh-hat story in a fairly straightforward manner, noting that in "any other political climate" the president's visit would be noncontroversial. Soon, however, the article put aside this sensibility, saying that his decision not to go "reportedly" had nothing to do with the Sikh faith, but that the determining factor, "apparently," was the dread of White House advisers that photos would spread virally. The article then cited precedents for such worries, including "fringe political theories" calling the president's U.S. citizenship into dispute, which "have stubborn staying power in the age of Internet conspiracy-mongering." A photo of the president in "foreign religious ceremonial gear" would provide "catnip" to such theories.

The basic question was how the president of the United States could possibly be required to wear a special hat, especially considering that ill-advised Americans often mistake Sikhs for Muslims. The president's decision, therefore, could be seen as an affront to Sikhs, not to mention Muslims, not to mention ill-advised Americans of other faiths, or of no faith at all. At this point Yahoo! provided a helpful link to a "related" story: MICHELLE OBAMA CRITICIZED FOR SUMMER VACATION.

The article went on to say, "It's unclear, at any rate, whether this sort of last-minute impression management can make much of a difference in a status quo that already has 1 in 5 Americans believing that the president is secretly a Muslim." Yahoo! then offered links to various other presumably related stories, including COULD 2012 DOOMSDAY PREDICTION BE WILDLY INACCURATE? and 10 FAILED DOOMSDAY PREDICTIONS and EARTH IN THE BALANCE: 7 CRUCIAL TIPPING POINTS and TOP 10 WAYS TO DESTROY EARTH, the latter of which linked to a story that indicated the Obama Sikh-hat thread was fraying: TOP 10 USELESS LIMBS (AND OTHER VESTIGIAL ORGANS). Not surprisingly, TOP 10 USELESS LIMBS linked to nothing; it was the logical, final destination of a journey that began with a discussion about President Obama potentially wearing an unfamiliar hat.

A subsequent Yahoo! News article predicted massive outrage over Obama's decision to visit a mosque in Indonesia, though his two presidential predecessors had made similar visits to Islamic holy sites while in office.

Given all of that, it's easy to understand the Obama administration's trepidation about the Sikh hat, assuming the administration did, in fact, cancel the trip for that reason. This is a new era of political news, in which a story can be fabricated out of whole Sikh-inspired cloth and become a legitimate part of the debate.

As Michael Hirschorn observed in *The Atlantic*, a few weeks before the 2010 midterm congressional elections, "When you enter the realm of politics and ideology, the distinction between opinion and fact starts to cloud, and the stakes become dauntingly high; there is no system of communal 'we' to rely on to hash out issues of the truth." The result, Hirschorn concluded, is that "the dislodging of fact from the pedestal it had safely occupied for centuries makes the recent disturbances in politics and the media feel like symptoms of a larger epistemological, even civilizational, rot. The next presidential election will, no doubt, be something to watch."

The truth is that were it not necessary to rely on incontrovertible, documented facts, opposition research would be—well, it would actually be a lot easier. We could simply report that a certain candidate had roomed in a fraternity house with someone who was later convicted of date rape or who had a close friend who was in the mob or whatever, and go from there. We could take the purchased narratives of disingenuous prostitutes as gospel. But because Michael and I are, at heart, journalists—agnostic in our assessments even as we're aligned with a political party—nothing matters to us that cannot be substantiated beyond a shadow of a doubt.

While we objectively investigate and report on the subjects of our research, what separates us from full-time journalists is that we never directly publish our political work (though I do publish freelance newspaper and magazine articles on other topics). As a result we have limited control over how it's eventually presented to you, if it's presented at all, much less how you will choose to receive it. Whether what truly matters will matter at election time is never clear until the end. Campaigns sometimes make bad decisions. Untruths go viral. Other issues come to the fore. Large numbers of gullible, ill-informed people flock to the polls. There are no guarantees. We've seen baseless attacks succeed, and we've found truly disturbing information that our campaigns chose not to use, which as a result never saw the light of day, ultimately to the public's disservice.

One of the most disturbing research reports we've done involved a candidate for mayor. We discovered evidence—an obscure newspaper interview, which saw no local coverage—concerning allegations that the candidate had molested two young gangsta wannabes whom he had taken into his home, ostensibly to help them. The boys had subsequently filed complaints with the local police department, the records of which had since disappeared, after which both young men were murdered. The cases never came to trial. We had no way of knowing if the candidate did anything wrong, but there was that one documented interview in which he acknowledged that he may have touched the boys inappropriately, and there was the issue of those police files that had mysteriously disappeared.

Our candidate chose not to use the information because it was so distasteful and squalid, and the opponent, the alleged molester, won. Over the course of his term, he took more errant boys into his home. He was eventually indicted on federal charges stemming from an incident in which he was riding around, allegedly drunk, in a police department RV, and along the way had, with a group of thuggish guys, taken sledgehammers to an occupied house, claiming it was a drug den, though he had no legal justification. By the time the mayor came up for reelection, he was done and the city government was in shambles. He ended up losing the election, was hospitalized with suspected heart problems on election night and died two days later. The story of the alleged molestations never came out. The voters never knew.

Even if a campaign uses our findings, and uses them judiciously, every community has its own threshold of tolerance for various affronts, and those thresholds are subject to change. Before the BP oil spill in the Gulf of Mexico threatened to destroy the local way of life, a region such as southern Louisiana, which is dominated by the petroleum extraction and fishing industries, might not have cared that an incumbent voted for appropriations benefitting an oil company from which he'd received large campaign donations. But now? That dynamic has changed.

Because the public tends to take a dim view of gratuitous attack campaigns, such information is often leaked to reporters who act as codependents and enablers—a relationship that sometimes leaves Michael and me, as erstwhile journalists, ambivalent. We've had a few awkward encounters with reporter friends while poking around in newspaper libraries, and the symbiosis can be tricky because reporters, if nothing else, like to think they discover the news. One of the mistakes the Mississippi businessmen made when they trotted out their prostitutes was not feeding their information to the media in a way that allowed the reporters to assume ownership, rather than to react with skepticism, which is every journalist's default setting. As a result, the media assumed ownership of a story about the political attack rather than the potentially damaging information on which it was based. Political campaigns have to consider the entire spectrum that oppo research will pass through, from the clerk at the counter to the campaign to the media and finally to the voters themselves. Self-centeredness, to the point that they deem something important simply because it seems important to them, or unimportant precisely because they don't care, will get them in trouble sooner or later.

In our experience, both inexperienced, unwary candidates and seasoned elected officials sometimes fall for the lure of questionable opportunities, for different reasons—one, because they're politically naïve, and the other, because they've grown complacent or arrogant. Learning about local communities helps us understand how a deed that would go unnoticed in one place will play big in another. In the Deep South, where manners are part of the local currency, being impolite may be more damaging than whatever rude detail you have to relate. A lot hinges on how the campaign delivers the news, if the campaign chooses to do so at all.

What's different about legitimate opposition research, as opposed to unfounded attack campaigns, is its factual basis and how the results come into play. Some campaigns may simply assign an intern or a volunteer to do perfunctory document reviews, then put the information out there for public consumption, but in the best cases the results of more exhaustive research are used to craft a cohesive, factual, negative storyline about the opposing candidate, and meanwhile to prepare for whatever negative storyline the opponent may craft about you. Everything, including the opponent's and your defense, is framed within that context. It's not so different from watching the video of your adversary in a boxing match, or a football game, to identify his strengths and weaknesses. Portray your political opponent as a liar, based on one documented event, and it's possible to throw everything into doubt.

Michael and I cling to the belief that if the truth is revealed it will prevail, but it doesn't always work that way. An elected official can repeatedly claim that he fought in Vietnam, when he didn't, and be reelected. Opposition research, even when it succeeds, sometimes fails. The fruit goes bad after it's picked or for whatever other reason just doesn't sell. One need look no further than Mississippi in 1983. As remarkable as the events of the state's gubernatorial election that year were, the outcome was even more stunning. Due to public revulsion over the conservative businessmen's attacks, the candidate—a white attorney general who'd been accused of having sex with black transvestites in a Bible Belt state with a notoriously conflicted racial history—won. Here was a cautionary tale about how wrong opposition research can go—how badly the practice can be abused and how utterly it can backfire.

Admittedly, some things were different then. The idea of attacking a candidate's personal life went against the tenor of the times, and the public's distaste over this violation of decorum seems dated today. People were also more easily shocked then than they are now, which is why the prurient nature of the attack made them feel as if their own privacy had been invaded. Yet the businessmen's attack campaign, and their candidate's inevitable embrace of it, broke a host of rules that still apply. One is that despite the bewildering success of sensationally false allegations in the blogosphere and on cable news today, it's still a good rule of thumb to avoid using hookers as your star witnesses—particularly if you also paid for their services, for whatever it was you were into (in this case you just wanted them to talk, which had no doubt been the case before). Second, it's always a good idea to make sure you can satisfy media scrutiny and that you have the immediate support of your own candidate. You want to control the story from the outset. There can be no questions about anyone's commitment to it. It's crucial to ensure that you, not the subject of the attack, will be the recipient of public sympathy. There are many routes to accomplish this, all of which involve knowing—*for real*—that the damnable thing you're about to say about someone is true, that it matters and that it can be proved.

If the voters decide to elect the guy anyway, you have no choice but to move on. That's democracy.

16

Michael

Given that the purpose of our work is to influence elections, you might think that one of its rewards would be the smug satisfaction that comes from watching an effective campaign commercial that's based on our research. Maybe we'd be sitting in a bar, drinking with friends, when an attack ad comes on the big screen, one for which we've laid the groundwork. We'd raise our hands, silencing everyone, and watch, rapt, as the soothing yet forceful voice of the narrator proceeds to ream our opponent a new orifice, based on true facts that we uncovered through days of dogged research and hours behind the wheels of low-horsepower, poorly sprung rental cars. The ad would be our splashy trophy ride. High fives, and a beer for everybody at the bar.

And yet. One of the quirks of our job is that Alan and I rarely see how our research is used. We never experience those great bar moments. Sure, we may come across a few bits and pieces—perhaps a TV ad, if it airs in our viewing area or comes up on YouTube, or a news release forwarded to us by one of our campaigns—but by the time the campaign season enters its final stretch, we've moved on. We turn our attention to other projects and monitor the campaigns from afar, much like any other voter.

One difference is that we don't just find the onslaught of campaign ads generally annoying, as most Americans do. Our audits don't stop after we receive our last campaign check. If we do watch those ads, whether they're aired on behalf of our candidates, their opponents or anyone running for office anywhere, it's with an informed yet jaundiced eye. We're keen for subtle distortions of the truth and outright lies, both of which are remarkably common.

Having done this since the early nineties, we've observed that during the last two congressional election cycles the attacks have become more pervasive and brutal, but more importantly, they rely less and less on documented facts. More money was spent on negative political ads during the 2010 midterm elections campaign than ever before, but few of the ads offered clues about their documentation. Because of that, it's hard to know for sure whether ads are becoming more or less truthful, but there's no question that many play fast and loose with far-brought, dear-bought facts.

For years I've associated campaign season—and the bombardment of early-fall ads it brings—with the state fair. They occur at about the same time and so I've always had a tendency to link the two. Growing up in Dallas, I had the largest state fair in the world basically in my backyard, and every year, one of the souvenirs my family came home with was a box of saltwater taffy. To watch it being made is an amazing process, with the baroque mechanizations of the taffy puller—three bars that rotate sequentially, stretching the looping taffy round and round. You first boil together all the necessary ingredients: sugar, butter, various flavorings and coloring (there is no actual salt water). This boiled concoction is stretched and pulled and stretched and pulled over and over again. Once it becomes fluffy enough, it's rolled, cut into bite-size pieces and wrapped in wax paper. Though the taffy looks tempting and tastes great, it is notoriously bad for your teeth. And too much can leave you feeling vomitous.

Campaign ads are often nothing more than political taffy. The ingredients—the facts gathered by researchers such as Alan and me—are mixed together and prepared for the machine. The media experts who create and produce the TV ads stretch and pull this concoction of information to its breaking point, and sometimes beyond. It's then cut into thirty- and sixty-second spots and presented to voters for their viewing consumption. They can be tasty for sure, but their nutritional value to an electoral diet is typically minimal. And if you're the one who churned the butter, refined the sugar and eagerly watched the process from beyond the window, you're likely to be disappointed.

When these ads are stretched too far, whether by sloppiness or by design, it's even more disheartening for us. Then the ads we watch can seem downright sinister, and we're liable to suffer a temporary loss of faith in the process in which we participate. We see errors, oversimplifications and outright fabrications. After all, people like us put in a lot of time to find the truth. Where did it go?

In one congressional campaign on which we worked, the opponent ran an ad that began with an empty overstuffed chair—the kind congressmen sit in during the session—to signify our candidate's supposedly poor attendance record and low success rate in getting bills through Congress. The point of the ad: Our guy wasn't there for you. He did not represent you well.

The ad had just enough of the truth to pass for it. It cited the relatively small number of bills our candidate had passed, which was true as far as it went. But laws with a congressman's name on them aren't an accurate measure of a congressman's success. Many of our guy's bills had been incorporated into other bills that were subsequently passed, without the original sponsor's name. In fact, he had an acceptable attendance record and did pass his share of legislation. When he spoke up about the ad, the opponent didn't back down. The truth had slipped off the screen, and the opponent saw no reason to retrieve it. The empty chair—an empty prop, no doubt borrowed from some media agency's stock photos—had served him well. Fortunately, the opponent lost anyway.

Voters often say they don't like all the negative campaigning, but liking isn't really the point. Would campaigns air so many attack ads if they didn't possess the potential to work? It's about impact, recollection, reinforcement, changing minds and getting people to the polls. Studies have reached many conclusions in that regard. They have shown that people who watch and remember negative ads are more likely to vote.

They have shown that negative ads are more memorable than positive ads when they reinforce a preexisting belief, that the impact of negative ads increases over time and that positive ads aired as countermeasures lack the same power. Negative ads can increase political participation particularly among those with the least amount of political knowledge. That's how you end up with an ad making the absurd (and, yes, untrue) claim that a senatorial candidate had supported taxpayer funding for Viagra for convicted child molesters.

The website FactCheck.org is a great source for verifying the authenticity of many ads and campaign claims. The trouble is, most voters don't fact-check, even when someone else has done all the legwork. In one case cited on the FactCheck website, a former New York governor's political group had made false claims in ads attacking Democrats over health care reform. The group launched two nearly identical ads criticizing Democrats in New Hampshire and New York for voting for the new health care law. The ad made several false and unsubstantiated claims, according to FactCheck, including that the law creates "longer waits in doctors' offices" and that "your right to keep your own doctor may be taken away." The group said those claims were about a Medicare payment program that the law calls for establishing, but it cited an opinion piece that doesn't make those claims at all.

The actual author of that opinion piece told FactCheck that it was "bogus" to cite his article as support for the ad. Even when an ad cites supposed documentation, it may be untrue, regardless of which party or group airs it. The ad also falsely called the health care law "government-run health care," when, in reality, the legislation will expand regulation of the insurance industry but build on the current private health care system and expand business for private insurers.

The group behind the ad, with the evocative name Revere America, is a 501(c)(4) organization, which means it doesn't have to disclose its donors. Revere America told FactCheck that it hoped to spend "several million" before Election Day in 2010.

Likewise, a slate of ads from the American Crossroads "super PAC" attacking Senate candidates in Colorado, Illinois, Ohio, Nevada, Missouri and New Hampshire made numerous misleading or false claims. One described an incumbent as having been "the deciding vote" on health care, though he was one of sixty senators who supported it. An Illinois ad misused a newspaper headline to imply that an incumbent was at fault for the loss of millions in a college investment fund, and a New Hampshire ad accused an incumbent of voting for projects that weren't even mentioned in the stimulus bill he supported. You get the picture. According to FactCheck, the American Crossroads PAC funded the ads under new regulations allowing unlimited contributions from individuals, unions and corporations.

"Distortions, stretches, half-truths and omissions are familiar features of political campaigns," the *Cleveland Plain Dealer* observed on October 5, 2008. "But independent fact-checkers and analysts say that outright falsehoods in candidates' ads may be reaching a level not seen since TV commercials entered presidential politics as the primary pipeline to voters in 1952." This meshes with what we've noticed, and it's happening, according to the article, "because false advertising works, because there are few, if any, penalties for it and because truth becomes a relative and disputable term in the alternate reality of partisan politics." In some cases, the *Plain Dealer* allowed, it is also happening because, as *Seinfeld* character George Costanza said, "It's not a lie if you believe it."

To its credit, the *Plain Dealer*, in partnership with other Ohio newspapers, meticulously fact-checked all presidential campaign ads running on television in the state. In the three months before the article's publication, the newspaper rated each ad on a 0–10 scale based on its truthfulness, whether it told the whole story, its fairness and its substance. At the time, the average score for "truthiness" for both campaigns was below a 5: The McCain campaign was 3.6, while the Obama campaign was 4.9. Eight McCain ads had received a zero rating, compared with one for Obama.

The *Plain Dealer* reported that PolitiFact.com, a project of *Congressional Quarterly* and the *St. Petersburg Times*, rated forty-seven McCain ads and statements as ranging from "barely true" to "pants on fire" false, compared with thirty for Obama (McCain had six ads in the "pants on fire" category; Obama had one). "Two McCain ads drew particular notice from fact-checkers," the *Plain Dealer* noted. "One said Obama's 'one accomplishment' was 'legislation to teach comprehensive sex education to kindergartners'—misrepresenting his support for teaching them about inappropriate touching by adults, and understating his record." Alan and I couldn't help but wonder how the researchers who gleaned what may have seemed like telling details from Obama's legislative record felt when the ad aired. Maybe they didn't care, but we definitely would have.

A number of nonpartisan websites systematically fact-check political ads, statements and campaign e-mails, including FactCheck.org, of the Annenberg Public Policy Center; PolitiFact.com; Fact Checker of the *Washington Post*; and the *New York Times*. Top sites for fact-checking e-mails are Snopes.com and UrbanLegends.about.com. Remarkably, some people believe that the actual fact-checkers are lying—that the process of vetting facts is itself part of a political conspiracy. Typical of this view was a reader post on the FreeRepublic.com website concerning FactCheck. org: "For the most part, they are just another extension of Democrat media bias." Others claimed that because Obama was ruled factually accurate more often than McCain, the fact-checkers themselves were clearly in his service. One post stated, "Factcheck.org is unquestionably a pro-Obama site. They even claim to have proof that Obama was born in the USA." You get the idea.

The *Washington Post* said in a 2008 front-page story that after becoming fed up over claims and falsehoods by the McCain campaign, including that vice presidential candidate Sarah Palin had said "thanks but no thanks" to the so-called bridge to nowhere, the Obama campaign broke a taboo and used the "L-word of politics to say that the McCain campaign was lying." That may have been true, but because it's impossible to prove intentional deception in such a case, calling the claim a lie was itself a stretch, according to the *Plain Dealer* article. Sigh.

Whatever the intent or term, false and negative political ads often work very well, and there's no one to regulate misleading claims, which is significant when more money is being spent on negative ads than ever before, and when the government has relaxed requirements to identify who's paying for them. By the time the ads begin to air, Alan and I are sitting mute at the bar. Candidates are no longer much concerned with media or public backlash, and, according to the *Plain Dealer* article, studies have shown that debunking falsehoods can actually reinforce them through repetition.

People screen out facts that run counter to broad narratives they accept, and they perceive reality in a way that conforms to their long-held beliefs, said science writer Farhad Manjoo, who writes about the phenomenon in his book *True Enough: Learning to Live in a Post-Fact Society.* "Indeed, you can go so far as to say we're now fighting over competing versions of reality," Manjoo wrote. "And it is more convenient than ever before for some of us to live in a world built out of our own facts."

By rebutting untruths, meanwhile, "a candidate departs from his own message and can risk being seen as weak or complaining," the *Plain Dealer* wrote. "Crazily enough, candidates have a legal right to lie to voters. The Federal Communications Commission requires broadcasters to run ads uncensored, even if the broadcasters believe they are false, and the Federal Election Commission deals with campaign finances, not ads." According to the article, Ohio has the toughest truth-in-political-advertising law in the nation, yet there are no fines or enforcement mechanisms.

Commercial companies are bound by restrictions that prevent them from making false claims about their products or those of their competitors. When they make such claims anyway, they do so at their peril, because they can be penalized by the Federal Trade Commission. Political candidates are not held to the same standard because their statements fall under the free speech protection of the First Amendment. *Time* magazine noted that certain states have attempted to establish their own standards for truth in political advertising, but without much success. Washington State passed a law in 1984 that made it illegal to sponsor campaign commercials that knowingly "make a false statement of material fact." Fines of up to $10,000 were possible for each instance, and violations could result in election outcomes being voided. "After fourteen years, the Washington State Supreme Court ruled the law unconstitutional, prompting one of the dissenting justices to complain that it was the first court in the history of the Republic to declare First Amendment protection for calculated lies," *Time* wrote. Even the normally staid magazine observed that the lesson to be learned from the effectiveness of baseless political ads is, in this case, that the truth is for losers.

Given all of that, it's probably just as well that Alan and I don't often see the results of our work, or that of other opposition researchers. As sticklers for the facts, and believers in the usefulness of the truth in determining who is most able to lead, we'd probably just end up crying in our beer.

17

Alan

Maybe it's a consequence of looking for the bad in everyone that now and then Michael and I start to wonder about ourselves. It's not a question of whether we have skeletons in our closets. Though I've never researched Michael, he certainly seems above board, and for what it's worth I once passed an FBI background check. The question is more fundamental about our work—whether we, as opposition researchers, are a positive force or just a pair of negative electrons bouncing around the political universe. Are we like the laughable Team Negative, the mindless political attackers on *The Daily Show*?

We're unequivocal about the importance of what we do. We've helped derail the political aspirations of unsavory or otherwise unattractive characters, and we believe the public has a right, even a responsibility, to know the truth about whomever they choose to lead them. But we do sometimes feel like troublemakers, questioning everything, expecting the worst. What does that say about us, and, by extension, about politics? And what might its cumulative psychological and karmic effects be? If we hone these sorts of skills, where might they take us over time? If we all focus relentlessly on the negative traits of our leaders, who'll be left to lead?

One of the more memorable cases for me was when we researched an elected official who also happened to be a friend of mine. We'd been hired to research a slate of candidates in a primary election, and when I found out he was among them I informed our campaign, with the assurance that our friendship wouldn't pose a conflict—that we'd research his strengths and weaknesses as diligently as we would anyone else's, including our own candidate's. It was just business. Yet as I began deconstructing my friend I felt nagging doubts, not about my ability to deliver, but about the ease with which I could turn the harsh light of judgment on a friend. Michael and I like to think of our work as illuminating, but there's no denying that we're attracted to the dark.

The same doubts followed a recreational encounter during a research trip in Missouri. It was a sunny Saturday in the small city of Liberty, and Michael and I were looking for diversion after a week spent probing the depths of an opponent's record. We eventually settled on the Historic Liberty Jail, which stands a few blocks away from the first bank that Jesse James and his gang robbed. The moment we entered the building that houses the reconstructed jail I felt that something was amiss. The anteroom seemed oddly formal, its decor more appropriate for a funeral home than the entry to a reconstructed historical site. Across from us stood four dour elderly men in suits beside a pair of closed double doors. I didn't like the vibe, and felt an impulse to get out while the getting was good, but when I turned back toward the entrance another elderly man stepped in front of me and very purposefully locked the door.

We'd seen the Historic Liberty Jail advertised all over town, and had thought it odd that the Church of Jesus Christ of Latter-day Saints owned it, but because we had a weekend to kill and were more or less following the Jesse James trail as a sideline, decided to stop by. There was no connection to James, but the jail was turning out to be memorable in that it took "tourist trap" to new heights.

Perhaps a dozen fellow captives milled about in the anteroom, dressed in de rigueur American vacation apparel—cargo shorts and t-shirts or colorful track suits with matching fanny packs, most of them clutching cameras, guidebooks and bottles of water as they warily eyed their surroundings like cows in a catch pen. Unlike corralled cows, however, their response was not to trot around, bawling, but to stare at the floor. Only Michael and I were overt in our dismay.

Before I could suggest to Michael that we insist that they let us out, one of the elderly men stepped forward from his station beside the double doors, welcomed us to the Historic Liberty Jail and launched into a spiel about Mormon pioneer Joseph Smith, whom he described as a prophet who'd been held in the original jail for five months, during which time he had received three revelations that were recorded in the Doctrine and Covenants, etc. I can't say why Smith was incarcerated because I tend to be averse to doctrines and, to a lesser extent, covenants, and after I heard the word "prophet" I stopped listening.

I have a visceral reaction to unsolicited proselytizing, which I attribute to having been subjected, throughout my youth, to the relentless intermediation of a Southern Baptist church. I once encountered a street preacher in the New Orleans French Quarter who demanded to know how I'd feel if Jesus returned to find me in that den of sin, to which I responded that I thought Jesus, of all people, would feel right at home in such a place, where life, with all its attendant searches, was in full view. My personal theory is that many stalwart Christians would be chagrined if Jesus showed up at their church on a Sunday morning with his retinue of radicals and at least one suspected prostitute, wearing a sweat-stained robe and long, infrequently washed hair, and proceeded to stride to the pulpit as if he owned the place. Someone would dial 911. Jesus would look nothing like a telegenic congressional candidate, which, despite the stylized paintings illustrating this, would come as a huge and unwelcome surprise to many in the congregation. As I explained this, the street preacher stared at me blankly, then waved his sign at someone else passing by. Maybe the self-righteousness inherent in the Southern Baptist church had not gone away, but had simply taken a different form.

I actually do believe in prophets, and that Jesus was one, but I don't appreciate someone else attempting to commandeer the vetting process. Perhaps if Michael and I had been researching the Mormon church and its authoritarian theology we might have felt differently that day in Missouri, but we were not up for it. So as the old man droned about Zion, I interrupted to state my desire to leave. Turning to the man by the door, I added, "Unlock the door." I should have said please, but he had stepped in front of me to lock the door, which, in my view, suspended the rules of decorum. Plus, I was a little pissed by the bait and switch.

The speaker stopped, midspiel, and stared at me. A few heads turned. Michael, who'd been brooding conspicuously but silently beside me, stood up a little straighter. Finally the old man at the front said, simply, "No." His tone was calm and assured, carrying the authority of an evangelical church that owned the building in which we were standing, the exits from which were locked. "This is part of the tour," he added.

"Let us out," I repeated, and, as an incentive, moved toward the old man blocking the door. "Unlock the door," I reiterated, and Michael nodded in agreement. Glancing behind me, I noted that the crowd appeared conflicted. Certainly, by now, they wanted out, too, but they were uncomfortable, as a group, with this breach of protocol. The men were old, after all. They wore suits. Michael and I were comparatively more threatening. No one moved to join in our mutiny. This, I've observed, is often how it works. Faced with an opportunity to think for themselves, which requires the gathering of one's own intel, and then taking appropriate action, most people's default setting is to go with the flow.

I once traveled with my friend Fe from Turkey to Bulgaria on a train called the Balkan Express—a euphemism for disaster, if ever there was one. At one point, for some unknown reason, we were forced to disembark in the middle of nowhere. I don't even know what country we were in. One minute we were sitting in our sleeper car wondering why the train had been stopped for so long, and the next we were dragging our wheeled baggage down the railroad tracks, strangers in a strange land. We were part of a group of similarly ejected travelers, suddenly and inexplicably on our own. We were disoriented, and could only hope that we were headed in the right direction, toward some manageable social framework.

A few miles later we came upon a town, and Fe and I decided to look for a bus station, but we couldn't read the signs and found no one who spoke a language we knew. As we crossed a busy intersection the light changed and we were forced to run the rest of the way through a flood of cars and trucks, dragging our infernal bags. After we reached the curb on the opposite side I heard continuous car honking in our wake, and looked back to see that the entire group of perhaps thirty ejected travelers had run out into traffic after us. Pandemonium ensued as cars swerved around them, and when the group reached us on the other side an Australian backpacker asked me, rather indignantly, "Where are we going?"

I said I had no idea, to which she responded, "Then why are we following you?"

I told her I was wondering the same thing.

In hindsight, the answer was obvious: They were following me because I was ahead of them, which is no way to choose a leader. Following someone simply because they're out in front is never a good idea, but it happens all the time.

In all honesty, after I'd been haphazardly selected I actually enjoyed leading our little group through whatever town it was, toward who knew what end. It felt good to be in charge. That's how politics works. Whether by design or through serendipity, an opportunity presents itself and someone picks up the ball and runs with it. I like to think I'd have relinquished my role to someone better equipped for the mission, but it would likely have depended on who it was and, well . . . it would have depended on a lot of factors.

These little episodes are the stuff of which big episodes are made. It's how someone who leads a group discussion in a college poli-sci class ends up being a forty-year veteran of Congress, growing rich in the process, and perhaps comes to see himself as immune to certain rules. We expect our leaders to obey the rules, not to lead us blindly into dangerous zones or into worlds that are otherwise not of our choosing. Yet we aren't always discerning in our selections. Sometimes we're just following them because they're there.

The leading old man at the Liberty Jail seemed to recognize that I posed a threat to the order of things but had not yet upset it. The crowd consensus was still to go with the program, rather than with the rude guy, so he grudgingly nodded to his counterpart by the door, indicating that I was to be released. I watched as a very clean, wrinkled hand reached down and unlocked the door, though it stopped short of actually turning the knob; I had to do the last part myself. And so the standoff ended. Michael and I stepped forth into the bright sunshine of Liberty.

"That was bullshit," Michael said, laughing, as we walked back to our rental car. Though I agreed, and was glad to be free, I felt a bit chastened by the exchange. I felt more like a troublemaker than a seeker of the truth.

Yet whatever our work says about us, and however ephemeral our knowledge of individual candidates may be, the documents we compile are informative outcroppings of history. It's not that history will necessarily care how a certain failed congressional candidate once contradicted himself. It's about how the political process is influenced, and how it evolves. Michael and I are focused on the forensics, on the irrefutable evidence of what is known to have actually happened—on the details of "current events," in the vernacular of a seventh-grade civics class. We never know whether our findings will have a long-term impact, but they often matter in the short run, and political history is, if nothing else, a string of overlapping short runs. Because our work is fact based we like to think it's more authentic than much of the political discourse, that only the act of voting is more simple and straightforward. We traffic in the raw materials of politics, before it gets spun and cropped and tested and put on the airwaves and on YouTube and, finally, debated during the run-up to the election.

After years of intensive, highly specific study of everything that can go wrong in the political realm, it's easy for us to understand why some people are attracted to good-looking, smooth-talking candidates who pose with their families against comforting backdrops, such as a neatly groomed suburban flower garden. So much about the world is dirty, unpredictable and harsh. Politics can be ugly. The danger is in allowing yourself to be sucked through the shimmering portal, to disregard the uncomfortable truths that hover close at hand.

None of this means that a candidate who does something wrong cannot be forgiven. Even when it seems unseemly to publicly disclose someone else's wrongdoing, negative politics can be a positive force for change. It all comes down to the gravity of the offense and how the offender responds to public disclosure. Once, while researching a congressional candidate, I was waiting in line at a local sheriff's office to see if the candidate had a criminal record (they rarely do, but we have to check anyway). Before me in line was a young man wearing frayed jeans and a t-shirt with CAMP FALLUJAH printed across the back. Notably, he also wore a hospital bracelet and had bandages across both wrists. When he approached the window he greeted the clerk cordially, and said, very calmly and quietly, "Afternoon, ma'am. I'm here to pay my fine."

The clerk, sitting behind a bulletproof window, glanced at the bracelet and the bandages and said, "Did you just get out of the hospital?" When he nodded, she added, "Should you even be up and walking around?" Again he nodded, but said nothing more.

Clearly, he was having some hard times, and I felt a little ashamed when I was called to the next window and had to announce, within earshot, that I was checking on someone else's criminal record. I felt strangely as if I were the guilty one, preying on the foibles of others.

As it turned out, the candidate had no criminal record, though in another office I would find that he had failed to pay state income tax—which, again, gave me pause. The same thing had once happened to me as a result of a clerical mistake made by the state tax commission. But as I followed the Camp Fallujah guy out the door, it occurred to me how easy it is to make a mistake, and to get caught, and how hard things can become afterward. If the Camp Fallujah guy were to someday run for elected office, and Michael and I were assigned to research him, whatever infraction he was guilty of would be highlighted in our report, no matter what other good he had done or how he later redeemed himself. I like to think he'd be the first to admit his mistake, and that the voters would properly weigh it in the balance, but the only way to ensure that the voters knew what they needed to know would be to document the facts.

When politicians are confronted with their mistakes, a good template for responding would be, "Afternoon, ma'am. I'm here to pay my fine." Unfortunately it rarely works that way. It's the secrecy, the air of entitlement, the evidence of chronic abuse of power, the not learning, and the lack of recognition that others make mistakes, too, that make powerful errors so loathsome. Michael and I are part of the system trying to influence voters, positively or negatively. We lay fires—a potentially destructive force, though we don't actually strike the match. If enabling the destruction of something bad can have a salutary effect, yet such an outcome is not assured, what, precisely, does that make us?

The problem, again, is that so much of American politics today is characterized by methodical distortion of the truth, which is how you end up with a candidate such as the one in Delaware who defaulted on her mortgage, lied about her education and dabbled in *witchcraft*, for God's sake, yet managed to win the primary by hurling unfounded accusations and innuendos at her opponent. It's bewildering, but it's no excuse to not care, or to allow yourself to be fooled. Attempting to undermine a candidate using irrelevant facts is to rely on a logical fallacy; like saying a candidate is a womanizer, and that therefore his position on balancing the budget is suspect, which doesn't naturally follow. If the same candidate has filed for bankruptcy, and his own business has been sued for nonpayment of bills and has had tax liens filed against it, it is logical to question his views on the budget. If he is a womanizer who uses his power to harass female staffers and to kill legislation aimed at equal rights, or both, then you've got something. It's not about who is most clever at insulting the other (at least, it shouldn't be) or at assassinating character in ways that have nothing to do with the ability to lead. It's about recognizing when bad traits have ramifications for the job the candidate seeks.

If, as a voter, you find yourself unsure, you can always search for the truth on your own, and you should feel free to shoot the messenger when it's clear that he or she is engaged in obfuscation. Don't fall for the kind of ruse presented by a certain vice presidential candidate who, after having lost her bid, publicly attacked the Associated Press for fact-checking her political record, as if that were an unreasonable invasion of her privacy. If you're putting yourself out there to lead the nation, your history matters—pretty much all of it.

The process of discernment isn't always easy. During the research trip when Michael and I escaped our captors at the Liberty Jail we were following tandem routes—the paper trails left behind by the candidates we were researching and the historic trail of the outlaw Jesse James. During the course of our research we'd repeatedly come across the ghost of James, who occupies a strange niche among American icons as a beloved murderer and bank robber. Most people are attracted to him. Brad Pitt played him, right? Yet he *was* a murderer and a thief.

As Michael and I compared the misdeeds of the various outlaws and lawmen on the Jesse James trail and, simultaneously, of the prospective outlaws and lawmen running for Congress, we liked to think our practiced critical eye enabled us to tell who was good and who was bad. But at times we found ourselves rooting for James. We discovered that we respected one of our opposing candidates more than the one who'd hired us.

Our misconceptions about James were a direct result of popular myth—something that also influences political campaigns. Our misgivings about one of our own candidates illustrated that we could remain objective even when it went against our political affiliations.

As we traveled from Missouri to Minnesota, along these tandem trails, we faced the same question again and again: Who, among the key players, was an outlaw and who was a lawman? As we sauntered into Northfield, Minnesota, and the old First National Bank, where Jesse James's gang was shot to pieces during a robbery gone bad more than a century before, we encountered a guide dressed in period Western garb. He was speaking with a small clutch of tourists who'd assembled to walk through the restored bank, the vault of which a teller had refused to open for the outlaws in 1876. Angered by this act of defiance, a gangmember had stuck a gun to the teller's head and blown his brains out.

The guide directed us to join the group and said he would shortly commence the tour, but we demurred. "You know, we don't really do the tours," Michael replied, slowly shaking his head with the pained grin I'd seen so many times before. The guide, who wore a cowboy hat, indoors, looked confused. His expression demanded some sort of explanation. "We're here on business and we really don't have a lot of time, so if we could just go ahead inside that would be great," Michael added.

Abashed, the guide protested that we might miss something without the guided tour.

"I think we'll be fine," Michael said, already walking past him. "We're pretty familiar with Jesse James." Always the dissidents.

There's a reason that Michael and I almost never take guided tours. It's the nature of our business that people are always trying to guide or otherwise influence our process of discovery, and we naturally resist, even recreationally. By this point, anyway, we'd become extremely familiar with Jesse James. Almost by happenstance we'd found ourselves at his birthplace in rural Kearney, Missouri; then in Liberty, Missouri, at the site of his first bank robbery and now in Northfield, the site of his last bank robbery attempt. We tend to notice when coincidental discoveries and random clues start to line up—it's a big part of our work—so we'd decided to run with the James Gang theme.

The political campaigns we work for take us down their own sets of trails. Some are longer than others, some are smooth and productive, some are borderline dangerous and some are simply frustrating to traverse. The same must have held true along the various trails the James Gang and the lawmen who pursued them traveled. In both cases, however, the lines sometimes become blurred. Outlaws and lawmen cross boundaries, and it may become difficult to tell the good guys from the bad. The truth isn't always found at the end of the trail, but when it is we usually have a beer.

On the final stop of this particular Midwest tour we visited the small, clapboard house in St. Joseph, Missouri, where James last lived and where, ultimately, he was shot to death by one of his own men in 1882. We'd finished our work for the day and decided to stroll around the homestead, where we came upon an exhibit documenting the 1995 exhumation of James's body, which put an end to long-standing rumors that he had lived out his life incognito.

"They dug him up," Michael observed, with some satisfaction. They'd gone to the source, to literally unearth the facts. It turned out that the man buried in the grave actually was James, so in a sense they didn't find anything they already didn't know. As research projects go, it was something of a wash. But it confirmed the truth. The circumstances of his death, as previously reported, were now officially fact, which is saying something, in our book. And make no mistake: Despite the popular spin, and the possibility that he was good to his mother, Jesse James was, on balance, a very bad man.

As we moved to the wall of the house where James was standing when he was shot, which still bore its fateful bullet hole, Michael wondered aloud whether they'd found the actual bullet—a natural question for someone who makes his living poring over shreds of telling evidence. Then, as we silently stared at the bullet hole, his cell phone rang; he answered, listened, muttered a few uh-huhs and said, "We can be there next week." He hung up and looked over at me. I didn't even ask where. It was time to move on.

Michael and I fervently believe that the voters need to understand the sources of the information that guides the political discourse, and we like to think we're uniquely positioned to help them do that. It helps that we both love hearing and telling stories, and that during almost two decades spent traversing the American political landscape we've uncovered countless tales that are interesting, illuminating and, in our view, important. Once we started working on this book, friends and associates occasionally asked if we weren't fearful that given the clandestine nature of our work we might become professional pariahs after it came out. It is something we'd thought about, but ultimately we wanted to tell those stories, and along the way, to highlight the fallacies of undertaking undocumented political attacks.

When we began pitching the idea of this book, a few publishers immediately envisioned a tell-all account, full of boldfaced names, and were disappointed to find that wasn't what we had in mind. We aren't here to name names or to reveal confidences, but instead to relate stories that we think say something bigger and more fundamental about politics and America. It isn't always about good guys and bad, but a candidate's record matters; it's the necessary underpinning of the debate, which need not be derisive for its own sake. Choosing an elected leader should not be like speed dating, nor should it resemble a criminal lineup. It should be a careful consideration of documented facts. And after the work is done, it's best to accept the outcome, to consider how the playing field has changed, and to reassess what you might look for in a leader the next time around.

In the case of that prickly campaign issue involving the candidate who was my friend, and the question of what our research of him said about us, the answer came when I felt obliged to tell him what had happened, though carefully, so as not to betray our campaign. He was gracious about it. "No problem," he said, not even bothering to ask what we'd found, perhaps because if it had mattered it would have likely already come out. With a laugh, he added, "Next time I'll let you know I'm running early on, and you can work for me."

18

Michael

For one minute I find myself just staring at the text message that's popped up on my phone. It's only a few words, a single sentence, but it has stopped me cold.

"Can you tell me exactly what you do for a living?"

It's a question that Alan and I often get, but rarely answer to anyone's satisfaction. It's a little difficult explaining exactly what we do, and even harder to describe why we do it. Sometimes we say simply that we work in politics, or help on political campaigns, or do research for political candidates. Most times, it's enough of an answer to ensure that there's not a follow-up. Most times.

But this is different. The reason my eyes are locked at this moment on those eleven words is that the message I've just received is from my teenage daughter.

She's on her way to meet the parents of her new boyfriend and she understandably wants to be able to tell them about her father and her father's job. It's a little different than just being able to say that your dad's an insurance salesman or a lawyer or a teacher. Those don't really require much explanation. But an opposition researcher? So I just sit with phone in hand and wonder why, after all these years, I had never fully explained my work to her and to my son.

Maybe I thought they wouldn't understand. Maybe I was worried they would see my work as sketchy. Maybe I felt they would be embarrassed. I love my job, and I have never placed much import on other people's opinions of it. But these were my children. So as they grew up, I just never discussed it much. After all, part of what makes Alan and me good at our job is an ability to stay in the background. We had always been most comfortable as outsiders on a trail, never really having to define ourselves as good guys or bad guys, never having to really align ourselves outside the realm of the broader venue of the Democratic Party itself.

Her message arrives one afternoon toward the end of a long campaign season—a season that has not only raised a daughter's question to a father's consternation, but one that, for Alan and me, appears to be our last together.

We have both been directly employed by politicians in the past, and we've occasionally been offered full-time political jobs during the course of our research projects. But for eighteen years we've continued to operate on the fringes, on our own, without conventional jobs. It's great being independent, and I suspect we work harder than a lot of people who enjoy the seeming security of regular jobs. But we've always both known that if either of us was offered the perfect professional segue, our alliance might end, and midway through a project in the Northwest it looks like that may finally happen.

The Oregon Coast is a supremely beautiful place, and it's refreshing to be doing research in a series of pleasant, progressive cities. But as we travel the highways south from Portland through Salem and Eugene and back up the windswept coast, Alan has other matters on his mind. He's debating whether to accept a high-level federal job that's been offered to him, and as a result he's frequently fielding calls from White House aides. While I'm inside a series of courthouses plowing through records, Alan's standing out front on the phone. The job is a presidential appointment, and is really too good to pass up. It's sad to think that Oregon may be our last foray into the field as a team.

"So, what do you think?" he asks me over lunch. "What do you think I should do?"

Of course there's some hesitation. After all, we've worked together for two decades, first sitting across a newsroom as reporters, then as business partners, traveling thousands of miles together on a road trip that seemed to never end. Even when we were working in separate places, it always seemed we were riding together in a crappy rental. I recall a June evening on the road, solo, for a U.S. Senate campaign, traveling from Dodge City, Kansas, to Kansas City. One of those nasty Kansas storms had blown up during the drive, with winds to seventy miles per hour, reports of twisters and the most amazing lightning display I'd ever seen. As I approached the city, talking on the phone with Alan, an incredible bolt illuminated the sky, striking a nearby storage tank that held fifty-eight thousand barrels of unleaded gas. It was startling and my phone actually crackled as the humongous fireballs roiled upward. Though he was six hundred miles away, my first instinct was to say, "Holy shit! Did you see that?"

Sure, we can irritate one another, but in a world of discontent where nothing seems to last, our biggest disagreements usually center on where to eat. We don't socialize with each other much when the campaigns end, and each of us maintains separate sets of friends. But no one knows us any better than we know each other. The thought of going it alone is, well, a lonely one. But for Alan it's an exciting possibility, offering the chance to participate in the political process at a high level, on the inside. For a writer and a researcher, the possibility of being granted such unimpeded access is seductive. It would be the ultimate research project.

"It's a great job. And I'm pretty sure that if I were in your shoes, I'd do it," I say. But I can't resist one caveat. "From now on, you won't be out there on your own."

There's nothing wrong with being with somebody unless you pretend you aren't—unless you're posing as an objective reporter or an honest elected official when you are secretly beholden to someone, or unless, deep down, you see yourself as being aligned with no one. It becomes glaringly apparent that there's a huge difference between being sort of with somebody, for a while, such as during a summer campaign, and being very much *with* somebody in a high level of government. Maybe Alan had forgotten how it felt.

The issue, in a way, has been a subtext of all our research projects. As independent researchers, we tend to be viewed as useful resources who are potentially beyond anyone's control. The majority of what we find is public domain. We are bound by campaign confidences, and we know everything that's potentially damaging to a campaign. We are both valuable and potentially menacing. With few exceptions, we research Republicans and Democrats, for Democrats. But in the end we *choose* to be leashed. The implication is that we could get loose at any time.

When our plane back from Oregon lands in New York late that night, Alan checks his e-mail to find a final offer from his prospective employer. It seems to contain everything he's asked for and now it's just a matter of accepting. As we jump into separate cabs, he tells me he needs to look it over one last time.

"I'll let you know something by Monday," he tells me. "But it's going to be awfully hard to say no."

I had the great fortune one summer to work as a mannequin repairman. It was by far the strangest job I've ever held, and without a doubt the most interesting. My friend Byron got me the position and together we worked in a Texas facility that received damaged mannequins from regional department stores, all in line for repair.

A brand new, high quality, fiberglass mannequin can cost hundreds of dollars. Prices have come down over the years with new production methods, but mannequins are still expensive, especially when a store chain might buy hundreds. So when they become damaged it can be more cost-effective to have them repaired than to buy new ones.

If you ever really take the time to look around a large department store you'll find that mannequins come in an incredibly wide variety. There are male mannequins and female mannequins; Caucasian mannequins and African American mannequins; baby mannequins and pregnant mannequins; headless mannequins and torso mannequins; bald mannequins and mannequins with molded hair; large-breasted, sexy mannequins and muscular, athletic mannequins; slender mannequins and heavyset mannequins. There are even translucent mannequins and mannequin "systems" that allow the owner to start with just the bust and mix and match different body parts.

The repair facility in which we worked held every type. And though they each seemed to be different in some way, they all possessed a common denominator: Every one was flawed. Maybe they were missing an ear or a finger or an entire leg. Maybe the joint that attached the arm to the shoulder was damaged so that the figure could no longer be placed into a waving position. Maybe they were just cracked or chipped or bent. So many things can happen to a mannequin to make it unattractive to shoppers. Our job was to make them attractive again.

To walk into a room of people donning surgical-type gowns and masks holding manufactured body parts in one gloved hand and sanders or glue or paint brushes in the other might seem a bit unusual. But we mostly took it seriously. Working with fiber glass required us to wear the protective clothing and, in a weird way, allowed us to feel like surgeons, albeit half-assed ones. Spare and replacement arms and legs lay in various parts of the facility like piles of amputated limbs left by battlefield doctors during the Civil War. We worked hard that summer, but try as we might, some mannequins were simply beyond mending. Their usefulness over, they were stripped for parts and cast aside. Mannequin repair is a cold and unfeeling business.

At the end of each day, every mannequin in the process of restoration was placed in its own open-faced locker. The eeriness of walking into work each morning before the lights were turned on to see a row of lifeless, naked figures in various poses and stages of repair, staring blankly back through the dimness, was something I took with me when I left—along with a gold translucent torso of a woman that lit up when I plugged her into the wall.

The mannequins we repaired that summer also left, back to the floors of the department stores from which they came. And though now temporarily free of defects, the truth is that the shoppers who pass by and maybe stop for a moment only really care about what's on the outside—the image that the mannequins present, the packaging that envelops them, the illusion that what is seen can somehow transfer to real life.

And so it is, as the first Tuesday of November rolls around and a long campaign season nears its end, that the shoppers who are voters try to overlook the imperfections that have so skillfully been worked over to select a new batch of elected leaders. By now, Alan and I have long since finished our work, have found the flaws in these living, breathing candidates, and have more or less left the building. By now, it's rare for anyone from our campaigns to get in touch with us, even for last-minute follow-up questions or document requests. They're working to get out the vote and the voters are preparing to exercise their power.

It's always strange to us that the election utterly determines the value of our work, but the final outcome is beyond our control. So much has been invested, so much energy and money expended. Now it comes down to a roll of the dice. The next two, four or six years will be shaped by a small percentage of capricious voters—some who've taken the time to study the candidates' backgrounds; some who enter the voting booth and select the first name in each race, knowing nothing about any of them; some who vote religiously because they feel it's their patriotic duty, or who do so to cancel their spouse's ballot; some who've spent hours posting rabid comments on various websites, or who look out the window, see that it's raining and decide to stay home.

All those television and radio ads that pummel us in our easy chairs and cars for weeks. All that direct mail and e-mail that suffocates our mailboxes and inboxes. All those debates and newspaper articles and yard signs and angry blogs and charges and countercharges. Is it worth it? Does it tell us anything useful or meaningful? Is it all illusion, or is it real?

There's an old parlor game in which players are lined up in a row and the first person is given a written sentence to memorize and then asked to whisper it to the next person. The sentence is whispered to the next player, and so on down the line, ending with the last person usually blurting out some discombobulated, confusing version of the original message. The game is called "Gossip," but it always begins with a fact, and everyone usually gets a good laugh at the end. Alan and I represent the first players in that row. The facts we gather, the flaws and defects we uncover, are as pure as possible; each is documented, tied up in a concise package and delivered. We may be asked to make suggestions on where it goes from our hands and how it is used, but most times it just gets passed down the line. Everyone in that line, from the campaign manager to the pollster to the media firm to the candidate and all those in between, have a responsibility to keep those facts straight and accurate. Sometimes they do; sometimes they don't. There are, of course, the occasional dirty tricks and smear campaigns fabricated by the Karl Roves of the world, and they are the ones that make the most headlines. While integrity is the goal, don't be fooled. Every campaign wants an advantage, an edge, and they will reach and stretch and walk the line to get it and to make their candidates look great.

Is it illusion? Without documented facts, the only way to really find out is to put a candidate in office, hold your breath and see what happens.

Each campaign season starts with feelings of invincibility and excitement, and thoughts of what could be. And each one concludes in simple victory or defeat. Like everything in life, campaigns are stories—stories that are conceived, written and told over a period of a few months. The best storytellers are the most successful, and everybody involved in politics plays a role in unfurling those sagas. Comedy, tragedy, drama—it's all there. For us, each research report we deliver is a story unto itself and we write them as such. Start at the beginning of a candidate's life, work through every facet of his or her career—whether it be as a politician or businessperson or teacher or doctor or judge—and end with the race now being run.

"What's the best thing you ever found on somebody?" From those who know what we do, that's the one question Alan and I get most often. What they're asking, of course, is what's the *worst* thing we ever found. Best is often substituted for worst when it pertains to the pleasure derived from the misfortune or pain of others.

What's the best hit you ever saw in football?

What's the best fight you ever watched?

What's the best thing that could happen to bin Laden in hell?

For us, there is no best or worst thing. It's more a question of whether a candidate is solid or not, irrevocably flawed or not. Sometimes we find a silver bullet; oftentimes we don't. It's all the little pieces of shrapnel that add up to paste a candidate in a political campaign. It's rare that we find nothing usable, but it does happen, and when it's the opponent we're researching, finding nothing gives us fits. But when it's our candidate, finding nothing can mean finding someone who, for the most part, is beyond reproach, who keeps us inspired, such as the Midwest nurse who was a political neophyte, with nary one untoward detail in her background, who had dedicated her life to helping people and saw high office as a way to do more.

Our research of her was thorough, but our report was brief. She was a near-perfect candidate, we wrote. Nothing in either her personal or professional life that could hamstring her campaign. She was just a middle-class woman with a family, who spent her career serving others. Her opponent, on the other hand, was a crusty longtime elected state official who had angered and confused voters of both parties with her stances on same-sex marriage, school busing and creationism in schools. Forced to seek other political avenues because of term limits, she was slaughtered on election day by our newcomer nurse. Unfortunately for her and the citizens she served, a political tidal wave four years later pulled her under and cast her out of office, along with many others who simply shared the same letter beside their names.

But with all the negativity that surrounds our work, and political campaigns in general, to find a candidate such as our nurse restores a sense of the goodness about people. The blemishes that permeate everything we do are pushed aside for the moment when someone appears from seemingly nowhere and carries the day for all the right reasons. And maybe people like her are the answer to the question: What's the best thing you ever found?

Alan and I generally don't go to election night parties. They are for the candidates and their campaign workers, official staffers and supporters—people who are part of the concentric circles ringing the candidate, around which we have orbited rather obliquely for a time. One of the few events I attended was supposed to be a victory party for the governor for whom Alan worked at the time. I joined Alan there, and we watched, with growing dismay, as the numbers slowly, inexorably, stacked up against his boss. You watch the votes coming in, see the general drift against you and tell yourself not to jump to conclusions because things can change, can easily swing the other way, after the votes in certain counties and precincts are counted. But in this case the trend never varied. Everyone grew quiet as the evening wore on, standing with their little plates of bland shrimp and toothpick-impaled cheese. I watched on multiple big-screen TVs as the race and Alan's job disintegrated simultaneously.

"Until then, I had fielded a hundred calls in my office at the Capitol on any given day," I remember him telling me. "But the day after the election my phone rang, precisely, once."

He had learned, then, the perils of being with someone. All those supposed political allies were gone. The governor still had a few more months in office, but his reign was over, and Alan had to figure out what he would do next. As it happened, that was opposition research with me. It had been a good run.

If accepted, the job offer now before him would result in only a temporary position, like everything else in politics, like our fieldwork for campaigns, like any assignment for a journalist—like American democracy itself, a constantly changing, ephemeral state, lurching this way and that, evolving and embracing this and that, and then moving on.

When my phone rings on Monday morning, I brace myself for the moving-on part. I know the questions with which Alan has wrestled. Would taking a full-time political position in Washington, DC, mean that he had merely been waiting for the right moment to tether himself to someone? Is our view of the world—our roles as independent observers and gatherers of fact—more important than any job, however attractive that job may be? They are the same kinds of questions, in various forms, that anyone who seeks political power must also answer.

"Well, I may be making the biggest mistake of my life, but sometimes you've just gotta say 'forget it.' I'd have to give up too much—everything, really, and I just can't do that," he tells me. It pains him for many reasons, he says. He'll be disappointing one of the rare politicians he truly admires, someone who could withstand the scrutiny, who could, as he likes to say, lead the tribe, whom he'd have been proud to work for.

Still, he would have to not only give up opposition research, but relinquish his ability to chronicle the story of American politics through the pages of this book. He'd be required to cancel the contracts for this as well as books he's previously published. Though there is a slim possibility that he might be granted an exception, the administration's position is clearly stated in the offer letter: The job is contingent on his agreeing to get out of all of his publishing contracts, which, viewed from the administration's perspective, is perfectly logical. As Alan points out, if his job were to preserve the power of the presidency, would he be willing to risk hiring someone who planned to publish a book about researching the dark side of politics? He would not, especially going into a presidential election year. So he must ultimately choose whether to let go of his independence, and in the end, he can't. He decides to hold on to this strange alliance: him and me, sometimes working for, sometimes working against, all the while wondering why, with so much at stake, so many people don't care, or seem to care about the wrong things.

"So where are we going next?" he asks me with a laugh that is part resignation, part putting the job offer behind him and part looking forward to the road ahead.

Allegiances are strange animals. They define us. They guide us. They bring about both success and failure. They steer us down the paths of our lives. We used to pledge the most basic of all allegiances as children, and then stopped for the most part when we reached adulthood, as if we no longer needed that reminder of loyalty to God and country. But allegiances exist everywhere; they swirl thick around our heads, tempting us always to choose or to swat them away.

In Pearl, Mississippi, at the Lowry Rifles Camp of the Sons of Confederate Veterans, which meets in the fellowship hall of the small Central Independent Baptist Church, members begin their meetings with an opening prayer and then pledge allegiance to the U.S. flag, then to the Mississippi state flag, then to the Confederate flag, vowing their faithfulness to the cause each represents. Are such polygamous allegiances even possible? Can a person be loyal to two opposing views at the same time, to two opposing governments whose stances, right or wrong, resulted in the deaths of hundreds of thousands of people? It's not like having a Toyota Camry and a Ford Taurus in your two-car garage. You can't get behind the wheel of the U.S. Constitution on Saturday and slide into your support for the Southern cause on Sunday. Pick one or don't pick any.

Some allegiances are exclusive. When Republicans in the House of Representatives unveiled their twenty-one-page Pledge to America in 2010 to tell voters what they'd do if they took control of Congress that November, they actually rolled out nothing more than a pledge to others in their party and to the conservative tea party movement that had been wreaking havoc on mainstream GOP candidates. The pledge, which included commitments to extend tax cuts for the wealthy and permanently prohibit taxpayer funding for abortion, vowed to "honor families, traditional marriage, life, and the private and faith-based organizations that form the core of our American values." Some provisions even matched the hardened positions of the tea partiers. The point is that such pledges are not really promises to "America" and are certainly not intended to include everyone, namely Democrats in this case. They are tools to divide, to differentiate and to destroy. In a political debate during a heated campaign, what could be better than to wave around a sheet of paper, point to your opponent and say, "I took a Pledge to America and he didn't."

The preamble to the promise included a line that read, "We pledge to honor the Constitution as constructed by its framers." It included a line that read, "We pledge to make government more transparent in its actions, careful in its stewardship, and honest in its dealings." It also included this: "We make this pledge bearing true faith and allegiance to the people we represent." When I read that last line I thought, "Huh? What? Didn't each of those House members already make those pledges when, on their first day in office, they raised their right hands alongside every one of their colleagues and uttered the words, 'I do solemnly swear that I will support and defend the Constitution of the United States'"?

To advance politically, you have to be with someone, even if that someone is just you. Your allegiances have to be secure. Your actions must be beyond reproach. You have to care about nothing more than what advances you politically, because that is the source of your power, whether you intend to use it for your own gain or for the betterment of society and the people you serve. Every day, our elected leaders and would-be leaders are offered invitations to form allegiances—from giant corporations with deep pockets, from small business owners with shallow pockets, from seasoned political activists, from fringe groups borne out of the issues of the moment such as health care and immigration reform, from regular folks interested in nothing more than a good job and a better life for their families. The allegiances they choose can keep them in office, send them back home or even put them in jail. For these current and prospective officeholders, it won't take a lifetime to be defined. Alan and I can do it in less than a month.

So we forge ahead with our freelance audit of American politics, trying along the way to explain to curious friends, and to a teenage daughter, exactly what we do. We dig alone, knowing that the outcome of the races we're researching will be determined by the voters who, on their own, will decide who should stay, who should go and who should take the wheel. November brings a new slate of winners and losers, though the election process never really ends. People may tire of that, of the endless campaign, but change is healthy. It keeps the country moving.

For now, the polls have closed, the weathered yard signs have been yanked from the ground and tossed in the garbage and fresh oaths of office—new allegiances—will soon be taken. Yet quietly hanging in the wings like a perpetual shadow is the question that's soon to be asked once more: Who are you with?

Acknowledgments

Alan

When I arrived in Chicago in 1993 for my first oppo research assignment, I had some experience in exhuming buried facts, primarily as a journalist. I was familiar with the machinations of politics, having ended up there as a result of the Mississippi voters giving the heave-ho to my former boss, Governor Ray Mabus, which forced me to cobble together a hybrid career as a freelance writer and researcher. A former compatriot from the governor's office, Jere Nash, who had since become a political consultant, had contracted with Michael and me as his research bad boys, and Chicago was my personal proving ground. I am therefore indebted to Jere for his advice and for getting the postpartum career rolling, as well as to my first newspaper editor, Lee Cearnal, for teaching me how to get to the bottom of things, and to former Attorney General Mike Moore and subsequently, Ray Mabus, for initiating me into the political realm.

Next, thanks go to my friend and fellow writer Shane Dubow, whose idea it was to write a book about doing oppo (I was initially skeptical, but he persisted), and who offered guidance as Michael and I went about developing the concept. From that point we benefited from the insights and ministrations of our discerning and enthusiastic literary agent, Patty Moosbrugger, as well as the thoughtful, erudite and incredibly-easy-to-work-with Stephanie Meyers, our editor at HarperCollins. Finally, Michael and I remain deeply indebted—indentured, even—to the complicated, unpredictable and occasionally insane political system of the United

States, which provides all the raw material an oppo researcher or a writer could want. And while it should not be confused with anything like gratitude, I feel we must acknowledge the general drift of American politics today, toward political performances that chew the scenery and play to the peanut gallery, with reckless disregard—on both sides of the footlights—for the truth. That, more than anything, offers continuing inspiration to Michael and me to find out what's really going on.

Michael

Often I have to peer over my shoulder and ask, "How did I even get here?" The answer, of course, is found in the names of the many friends, family members and colleagues who led, pushed, cajoled, conspired, inspired and traveled with me to this place. It's been quite a party.

To begin at the beginning of my political beginnings, I owe gratitude to Kane Ditto, one of the great unsung mayors of Jackson, Mississippi, who allowed me to ply my fledging love of campaign research in his re-election bid so long ago, tasting victory for the first time. Jay Neel, political consultant and longtime friend, who always talked up our ability to get the job done, and who knows everything about the Gettysburg battlefield, which is reason alone to recognize someone. My downtown family who has been with me from the first chapter. Craig Noone, a bright ornament who left behind a spirit that will always be wtih us. And Kate Royals, our steely-eyed guardian of facts.

While I echo Alan's acknowledgements, I must thank Alan himself. With three books under his belt, he guided me along this boulder-strewn path, forced on numerous occasions to endure the phrase, "I'm stuck and I'm going to get a shot of tequila." By the time we're through, he warned, you'll be sick of reading your own words. He was right, so I just read his.

Great stories never grow old. Claudia Levy convinced me a while back that I possessed an ability to tell a good one—and never grew tired of listening. She was a life preserver in a hurricane. Johnny, Rick and Sam, my lifelong friends, have always just been there. My two kids, Michael and Joanna, each in their own way, inspired so many of the words and thoughts presented here, and have been my breath.

Lastly, I must tip my cap to the most conservative Republican I've ever known; a woman who had to reconcile a mother's pride that her middle son could actually write a coherent sentence with the realization that he had somehow become a Democrat. And this acknowledgment should be construed as everything like gratitude.

About the Authors

ALAN HUFFMAN has been a newspaper reporter; aide to a state attorney general and governor; partner in the political research firm Huffman & Rejebian; and freelance contributor to the *Atlanta Journal-Constitution*; the *Los Angeles Times*; *Lost*; *National Wildlife*; the *New York Times*; *Outside*; the *Oxford American*; *Preservation*; *Smithsonian*; and *Washington Post Magazine.* He is the author of three nonfiction books: *Sultana, Mississippi in Africa,* and *Ten Point.*

MICHAEL REJEBIAN has been a journalist and newspaper reporter in Texas and Mississippi; director of communications for the Office of the Mayor, City of Jackson, Mississippi; political advisor to the attorney general of Mississippi; and a partner in Huffman & Rejebian. He is a journalism graduate of the University of Mississippi.